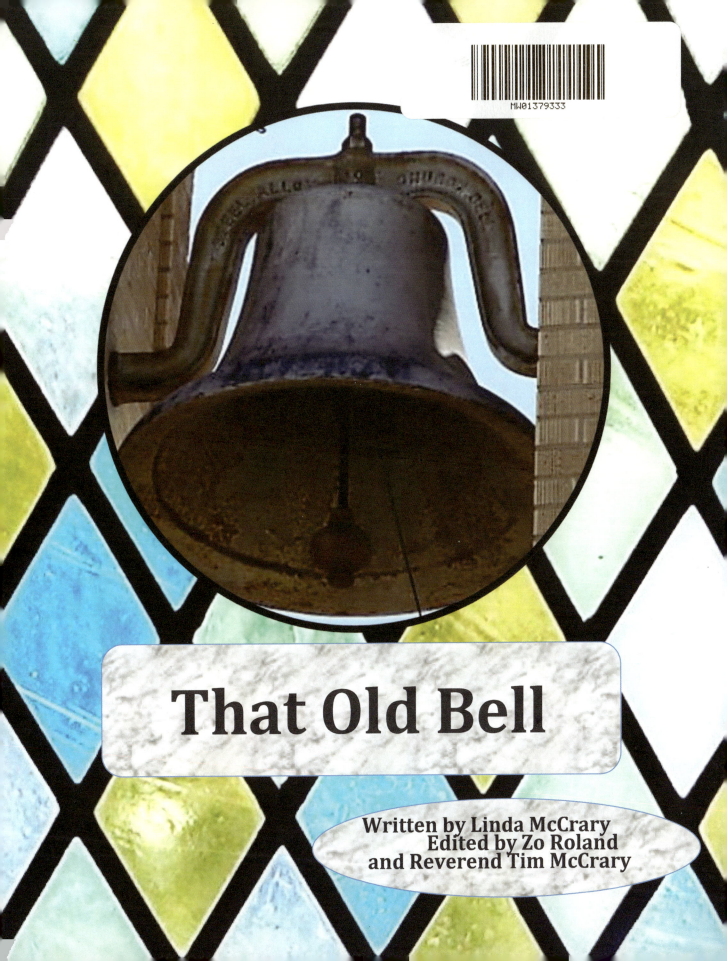

That Old Bell

Written by Linda McCrary
Edited by Zo Roland
and Reverend Tim McCrary

A year ago the first part of October, I was planning the 100 year celebration that we were going to hold on the first Sunday in November. In the course of that planning I had an idea that I would like to have a little magazine or pamphlet made about the last 100 years of the church. But I knew I would not have the time to put it together and began trying to think of someone who could when it dawned on me that I was living with the best person I knew who could do this thing. So I approached her with this idea, thinking that all she could say was no. But she not only said yes, she said it with such enthusiasm that I was amazed. Although when I asked if she could have it done by the date of our 100 year celebration she was not so enthusiastic. She said, "If I am going to do this, it is going to be done right!" Thank you Linda, for taking this hair-brained scheme and turning it into what it is.

Friends, here it is, the first 100 years of the old bell tolling, and a year out of Linda's life.

I pray it blesses you as it has blessed hers.

Pastor Tim

That Old Bell

This book is dedicated to those who came to Moscow, Kansas
in the early years and those who wanted a place to serve and worship our Lord.
And to you, friends, who are 2013 members, the "100 year members" of

The Moscow United Methodist Church.
Moscow, Kansas
who live and work to keep God's commandments, that this book is for.

But most of all "**That Old Bell**" is dedicated

to our Lord God

Because "through Him all things are possible"

AND ALL GODS CHILDREN SAID AMEN!

CONTENTS

Part I .... In the beginning

Part II .... The Little Frame Church

Part III .... The Basement Church

Part IV .... The Brick Church

Part V .... The Lord of the Dance

Scripture

Biography

Contributors to the publishing of That Old Bell

That Old Bell

"When I was young, I asked the Lord 'why are we here?'..."

IT BEGAN WITH A CALL TO COME AND SEE...

"Then Jesus turned, and seeing them following, said to them, "What do you seek?"
They said to Him, "Rabbi" (which is to say, when translated, Teacher),
"Where are You staying?" He said to them,
"Come and see.""
John 1:38-39

AND A CALL TO FAITH,

"Let not your heart be troubled; you believe in God, believe also in Me."
John 14.1

A CALL TO SERVANTHOOD,

"And Jesus came and spoke to them, saying, "All authority has been given to Me in heaven
and on earth. Go therefore and make disciples of all the nations, baptizing them in the
name of the Father and of the Son and of the Holy Spirit,
teaching them to observe all things that
I have commanded you;
Matthew 28:18-20b

AND A CALL TO LOVE.

"A new commandment I give to you, that you love one another; as I have loved you, that
you also love one another. By this all will know that you are
My disciples, if you have love for one another."
John 13:34-35

"When I was young, I asked the Lord 'why are we here?'
and He told me "To love your neighbor"

And, so it began:

Part I

That Old Bell

*"For where two or three are gathered together in My name,
I am there in the midst of them."*

Matthew 18:20

The dust storms or the "Dirty Thirties" as they are called, had not yet begun. The RMS Lusitania would not go down for another two years sparking America's entry into World War I. Woodrow Wilson had just begun his presidency and Henry Ford had just developed the first moving assembly line, creating the affordable automobile as well as many jobs.

The population of the United States had reached 97,225,000 (Consultancy) almost one-hundred million while the population of Moscow, Kansas a quaint 252. (ppt4web, 2014) Moscow, Kansas seated neatly between Liberal and Garden City, prospectively. It is a small town in the southwestern section of Kansas just trying to make a start in a new area 12 miles northeast of Hugoton along the newly laid Santa Fe railroad. According to Edith Thomson, Moscow got its name from the "abbreviation of the name Moscoso, who was an officer with Coronado's expedition that traveled through the southwest in 1541." (Stevens County History Association, 1979) The town's name originally spelled Mosco, had petitioned early on to receive a post office. When asked why Mosco was now spelled with a 'w' at the end, Joseph Rouse answered; 'a "higher power" at Washington, D.C. put the letter "w" on and the name has stuck.' Moscow received their post office and Anna M. Gray was given the privilege of becoming Moscow's first postmistress in May of 1913. (Stevens County History Association, 1979)

Moscow's first post office window can be seen at the Stevens County Gas and Historical Museum in Hugoton, Kansas.

Originally located about seven miles southeast, Moscow had decided to pull up stakes and move the entire town to its present location in order to benefit from the Santa Fe Railway which was in construction at the time. By being alongside the railroad, Moscow's growth and survival would be secured, as well as, giving the tiny town a spot in the running for county seat. It was very desirable at the time to live in a 'railroad town', and many people would move to railroad towns simply because a railroad ran through it. A railroad town meant visitors who spent money for rooms and meals. It meant new settlers, jobs, fairly easy access to goods, it meant you could receive news from other towns, and it meant you had voters. The coveted county seat created quite a bit of conflict, including what would become known as the bloodiest county seat war of the west. This 'war' left many men laying dead in an area known as the hay meadows, which was a neutral zone in Oklahoma on July 25, 1888. The Hay Meadows Massacre was a war between the men of Woodsdale and Hugoton over alleged lies to boost population numbers of one town. Moscow was not involved in this battle other than receiving some of the dead once it was over.

The county seat was not to be in Moscow's history books. Moscow lost this honor to the neighboring town of Hugoton. However, little Moscow, Kansas was not to be deterred from becoming a town and a town like no other. In a town meeting after Hugoton was named County Seat, after much bragging on the part of Hugoites, a Moscow man stood and announced "And Moscow is still here!"

With the railroad construction, the small town of Moscow moved buildings by horse and man to its new and present location. This was, as you can imagine, no easy task, but because of the lack of trees. Timber was not easy or cheap to find, consequently it was easier to simply move the buildings! At its new location, Moscow soon began to grow, businesses opened, and families moved in Moscow gained its post office, opened a bank, a hotel, pharmacy, and a grocery store, and even a restaurant, but, as yet, they did not have a church.

THE PRAYER OF JABEZ

And Jabez called on the God of Israel saying, "Oh, that You would bless me indeed, and enlarge my territory, that Your hand would be with me, and that You would keep me from evil, that I may not cause pain!" So God granted him what he requested.

1 Chronicles 4:10

Part II

Moscow Methodist Church

"The Little Frame Church"

November 1913 – February 1930

Pastors who served
Moscow "little frame" Methodist Episcopal Church
(Stevens County History Association, 1979)

1913 – Frank Henery Neff	1920 – Clayton Pearson
1914 – Elmer Lakey	1921-1922 – G.A. Parkhurst
1915 – J.W. Jones	1922 – Rev. Lewis
1915-1916 – B.L. Rudd	1923-1924 – W.H. Johnson
1917-1918 – F.F. Nixon	1925 – I.L. Neuenswander
1919 – C.M. McClure	1925 – E.A. Hull
1919 – T.H. Carson	1926-1927 – Oscar Matthew

Typically, Methodist churches began their ministry by holding Methodism classes in the homes of members. This may be the case in Moscow, however, Bolin and Hall's Hardware which was located in the town offered up their building as a meeting place. According to the Hugoton Hermes Newspaper dated March 7, 1913 The first *official* worship service, contrary to popular believe, was March 2, 1913 and was a huge success for the towns folk. (Hugoton Hermes, 1913) It was not long afterward that circuit rider T.B. Paramore, whose circuit included frequent visits to Hugoton, was introduced to the members and together with the town, began the work of

> ### MOSCOW.
> According to previous announcement, on March the 2nd the organization of the church was completed and a building committee was appointed. The first church service was held in Moscow, March the 2nd. The meeting was held in Bolin and Hall's Hardware building. There was a good turnout.
>
> C. C. Stull the leading merchant of Moscow has built a restaurant and Guy Pierce is running it for him.
>
> Charles Stutsman is making a new well near his residence in Moscow.

constructing the first church to inhabit Moscow, Kansas. Reverend Paramore had visited Hugoton along his circuit since 1904. However, while Moscow would not become a stop on his circuit Moscow townspeople were very appreciative and excited to welcome their first minister. By the end of 1913, Circuit Rider F.H. Neff was appointed to serve Moscow in his Ematon Circuit (Hugoton Hermes, 1913). The Ematon Circuit included the towns of Ematon, Pleasant Valley, and Wideawake together with the newly founded Moscow Methodist Episcopal church.

In November of 1913, the Moscow Methodist Church construction of "The little Frame church", would be completed at a total cost of $1,800.00 (Stevens County History Association, 1979) The beautiful bell was proudly hung in the belfry and made ready to ring out the call to *"Come and See"*. The towns of Ematon, located just east of Liberal, as well as, Wideawake, most likely located just northwest of Ematon, would accompany the many deserted towns during the Dust Bowl.

In June of 1917, Moscow signed the charter for their church. This charter officially announced the membership into the Methodist Episcopal Church Conference. Among those who signed this document of devotion, privilege, benefits, and responsibilities agreement were:

C.A. Stitt   R.S. Buddenburg

J.K. Hustand   Clark Coburn

C.M. Graham

With the first official minister, Circuit Rider Frank H. Neff (Stevens County History Association, 1979) and a beautiful bell in the belfry ringing, the Moscow Methodist Episcopal Church dedicated their service to the Lord in November of 1913. The "dedication of the church building" was celebrated with excitement, praise, and song with the voice of Ms. Lillie Miller singing a special song to the Lord. Ms. Miller would also sing at the dedication service of the second church, as well as, the third and present United Methodist Church.

The United Methodist Church
GREAT PLAINS AREA

9440 E Boston, Suite 160
Wichita, Kansas 67207
800.745.2350
Fax: 316.684.0044
www.greatplainsumc.org

SCOTT J. JONES
Resident Bishop

October 24, 2013

Moscow United Methodist Church
PO Box 96
Moscow, KS 67952

To the Congregation of Moscow United Methodist Church:

I am honored to add my word of congratulations to Moscow United Methodist Church as you celebrate your 100th Anniversary! For a century you and your predecessors have been reaching out to the community, growing in your ministries, and sharing the love of Christ with the people of Moscow.

November 3rd as you celebrate and recognize those who have served in your midst, I will keep you all in prayer. This day will bring past memories together with ones newly created, enriching your congregation's history and strengthening the Moscow UMC family for the future.

We Christians know that, when we celebrate our history and progress, we always are giving glory to God whose Holy Spirit leads us, guides us, and empowers us to become the people He has called us to be.

It is my honor to serve Christ *with* you in the Kansas West Annual Conference and the Great Plains Area of the United Methodist Church, and I wish you a powerfully blessed celebration!

Grace and peace,

Scott J. Jones

SJJ/lab

Kansas West Conference — Wichita
9440 E. Boston   800.745.2350
Suite 110   Fax: 316.684.0044
Wichita, KS 67207   www.kswestumc.org

Kansas East Conference — Topeka
4201 SW 15th St.   877.972.9111
P.O. Box 4187   Fax: 785.272.9135
Topeka, KS 66604   www.kansaseast.org

Nebraska Conference — Lincoln
3333 Landmark Cir.   800.435.6107
Lincoln, NE 68504   Fax: 402.464.6203
                        www.umcneb.org

This gasoline advertisement, was found in a March 28, 1921 edition of the Hugoton Hermes, you will note that gasoline was 20¢ a gallon! Today, 2014, the average gasoline price in Southwest Kansas is $3.45! That is a 1725% increase!

(right)

In the advertisement, coal oil (clear lamp oil that is similar to Kerosene) was 10 ½ ¢ per gallon.

(Note the phone number for the service station is 3 digits rather than the 10 digits today)

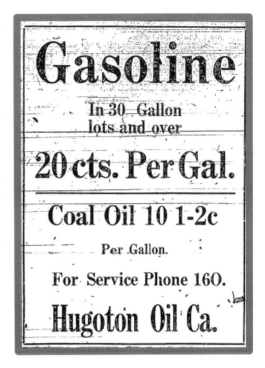

(The Hugoton Hermes, 1921)

"Coal Oil is Kerosene

The name "coal oil" is historically linked to Kerosene because of the common misconception that the Kerosene came from the coal. In fact, Kerosene comes from the oil inside the coal. The term "coal oil" is an outdated name which only flourished at the dawn of the oil industry."

(RexM, eHow, 2014)

(left) Grocery advertisement for Kinser Grocery in Hugoton from April 20, 1921 edition of the Hugoton Hermes. (note the phone number!) You will also see HELLO BUDDY! An advertisement for "TEN REASONS Why To Buy A CHEVROLET"

(Hugoton Hermes, 1921)

This is a page out of the 1916 - 1917 Sunday-School Record book. On this page is a list of the Sunday school teachers during those years.

REGISTER OF TEACHERS		
Name		Class
Mrs. Shaw		Primary
Mrs. Stitts	Asst. Ord Pearce	Intermediate
Mrs. Hiestand		Young Peoples
Mr. Stitts	Asst. H.E. McCue	Bible Class
	Alice Hoskinson	

This image tells the names of the teachers and the classes they taught according to the photo copy of the register.

This page of *BARTEAU'S Sunday-School Record* shows a chronological list of Sundays and a record of attendance with the class donations. On January 2, 1916 there were 20 students in attendance with a total collection of $0.44. By the end of 1916, two additional classes were added.

One year later on January 7, 1917 the total attendance was 27 and $0.75 was collected.
By November of 1917, the Sunday school attendance increased to an average of 48 students. Moscow's Methodist Episcopal Church was growing, and the bell in the tower continued to ring.

According to Ida Shriver's memories of Moscow Methodist Church in *"The History of Stevens County & Its People"* The photograph to the left is of the church congregation on the steps of the first Methodist Church, "the Little Frame Church". Some of the people pictured include: Mr. Franks, Mr. and Mrs. E.J. Stevenson, Virginia and Velma, Mr. and Mrs. O.K. Pearce with Lucile and Doris, Charley Dudley, Mr. and Mrs. Roll Buddenberg, Donna McCue, Mr. and Mrs. J. Mitchell, Mr. and Mrs. Lester Seger, Mr. and Mrs. Marvin Miller, diamond Caldwell and Melba, Muriel Brownell, Blanche and Gerald Gaskill. (Stevens County History Association, 1979)

In the early years, prior to central heat or radiators, one of the jobs appointed to the minister was to light the potbelly stove to heat the sanctuary prior to the church service. During the coldest months, it was sometimes necessary to light the stove a few hours before the congregation was to arrive for worship. This was not one of the more glamorous jobs, but a necessity no less.

There is a bit of controversy as to which church building this happened in, the Little Frame Church or the Basement Church. So to avoid making the wrong choice we will just say it happened in "the church".

In "the church" (wink, wink) the potbelly stove was located under the floor at the back of the sanctuary. In order to get to the stove, the minister had to move the last two pews far enough to clear a trap door which was under a rug. Once the pews were moved, he had to remove the rug to reveal the trap door, then finally, he had to pull the trap door up so he could go down the steps to where the stove was.

With the pews moved and the trap door opened, the minister would make his way down the darkened steps to the area where the stove and coal was kept. He would put the coal into the stove, light it, and then replace the trap door, rug, and pews before he could leave to get himself ready for services.

It was a difficult job, especially when there was only one person to do it. The pews were bulky and difficult to maneuver around, **however, it was a necessity during the winter months.**

According to Mrs. Miller, one especially cold Sunday morning when the preacher went to the church to get the heater going he opened the front door and was met by a no doubt, equally frightened…skunk! Evidently, someone with a nose for mischief had lured the skunk into the narthex of the church and shut the front door. It must have been done the night before possibly in the vane effort of getting to sleep in or for a good laugh when the congregation would have to wear clothes pins over their noses while the preacher delivered his sermon. As mentioned before, there is a little confusion whether this happened at the Little Frame Church of the Basement church, however, whichever building, it *'reeked'* of schoolboy pranksters looking for a good laugh!

Well, the skunk was released with well wishes and services went on as scheduled, no doubt, with a short announcement to whoever the jokesters were to please keep God's precious creatures in their natural habitat and out of the church.

The church had grown in "leaps and bounds" and was soon able to provide a more stable existence for their ministers. Typically, a minister on a circuit was provided with a hot meal, warm conversation, and a comfortable bed for the night. However, Moscow had been blessed so much the last 7 years that in 1920 the first parsonage was built providing the new minister a place to call home. The Reverend and Mrs. Parkhurst were the first to move into the new parsonage. They served Moscow from 1921 – 1922.

These days, the parsonage still stands in its original location. No longer used as a parsonage, the home was sold and various families have enjoyed the beautiful home built close to a century ago.

First Parsonage
Built in 1920
Occupied First By
Rev. and Mrs. Parkhurst, 1921-22

Rev. Parkhurst and family and Miss Kate Cromely were in Liberal Wednesday.

A number of folks met at the old Moscow schoolhouse Sunday afternoon and organized a Sunday School. Mr. Dan Cooper and family, Rev Parkhurst and family and D V Crosley and family were in attendance from Moscow.

Moscow News article found in the Hugoton Hermes

In 1921, Milton and Ida Shriver moved to Moscow township. Milton farmed then in 1928 they moved into town and joined the Moscow Methodist Church. Mrs. Shriver began teaching school. She was very active in the church and school until she passed away in 1990 at the age of 87. However, during her lifetime, she became much loved and her passing was mourned by the entire town. Ida Shriver was active in the ladies club of the Methodist church named the Ladies Aid, then the W.S.C.S. and finally the United Methodist Women.

Edith Campbell Thomson was another woman who was loved and respected by many. She was born on February 29th, 1888, in Woodsdale, Stevens County, Kansas. During her younger years she lived in Liberal, Kansas graduating in 1907. Mrs. Thomson was also a member of the Methodist Church as well as, a teacher in Moscow until her retirement in the spring of 1957.

"On Sunday, March 24, 1968, at the age of eighty, she was honored at "Edith Campbell Thomson Day" in the Methodist Church of Moscow. Her former pupils from all over the country came to share this day with her. She was presented with a scrapbook of mementos and pictures sent in by her pupils and by the community. A program of poetry, music and other tributes were presented. Edith was worthy of the honors accorded her. (Nina Wright Smith wrote a tribute to Mrs. Shriver titled Child of the Plains which depicted Edith Campbell Thomson and her life.)

CHILD OF THE PLAINS

(tribute dedicated to pioneer author, Edith Campbell Thomson, by Nina Wright Smith)

She was born on the plains of Kansas,
Lived her life with the wind and the sage.
The stories she tells us of Kansas
Could fill many and many a page.

We listen spellbound to the stories,
She tells of her life on the plains,
The sorrows, the hardships, the glories,
The growing and the harvest of grains.

Her life on the plains as a lass,
The schools as they were in her day,
The land that was mostly all grass,
The machines that were made to mow hay.

The land she watched grow as she grew,
It was changing even faster than she,
Till the land and the people were new
And the changes were marvelous to see.

What a joy it is that she shared this
With all who are willing to look,
In the pages of history we cannot miss
The stories she's told in her book.

(Stevens County History Association, 1979)

Mrs. Thomson was a prolific author, historian, friend and disciple of Christ. She was a native of Stevens county as well. Mrs. Thomson wrote *"Pages of the Southwest"*, *"The Lone Hill Story"*, *"History of Stevens County, Kansas"* among many other articles for the newspaper. (Stevens County History Association, 1979)

"Now it happened as they journeyed on the road, that someone said to Him, "Lord, I will follow You wherever You go."

Luke 9:57

During the early years of the church, one of the duties expected of members was to drive out into the community and outlining farms asking for donations to pay the bills including the preacher's meager salary. While asking for donations may seem like a difficult task, it never seemed to be a problem for the Moscow Methodists; many people were very happy to give whatever they could. Although, there were times when a neighbor was unable to donate more than a hot cup of tea and some wonderful conversation but that was okay as well as, welcomed. No one worried, they just trusted in the Lords favor to (Noob, 2014) supply the needs of the church.

"Then He said to His disciples, "Therefore I say to you, do not worry about your life, what you will eat; nor about the body, what you will put on. Life is more than food, and the body is more than clothing. Consider the ravens, for they neither sow nor reap, which have neither storehouse nor barn; and God feeds them. Of how much more value are you than the birds?"

Luke 12:22-24

The photograph below is a section of a much longer photograph. It was a popular method of taking photographs with panoramic views. A special camera was needed for these photographs. The camera was equipped with a lens that rotated along the film while the camera remained completely still. Another type of panoramic rotated.

This photograph of Moscow was taken in 1920. If you look close you will see the Methodist church steeple toward the back of the town.

Photograph provided by Stevens County Gas and Historical Museum, in Hugoton, KS.

(1920)

The "little frame church" had held many worship services, hosted numerous potluck dinners, fellowship gatherings, and provided an abundance of community services. The members of this small church witnessed loves united in marriage, babies baptized, and many "good-bye for a while" funerals. It also saw that the little church had become too small for the mission work that had yet to be done. God was far from finished with these faithful Christians who loved doing the Lord's work.

While considering options, the folks of Moscow reflected back on the past 27 years of service, and saw God's hand in many areas of their lives qualifying, equipping and enabling them to do His bidding. They also saw many changes between those years of 1913 to 1930, including;

Women's skirts going from there to here and back there again.
The 19th Amendment enacted, giving women the right to vote.
1917 saw America's entry into World Wars I when 1,195 passengers lost their life that fateful day that Germany sunk the passenger ship Lusitania
Another 116,708 more American lives would be classified as casualties of WW I
Prohibition took alcohol from American and the increase of crime came in its place.
Al Capone became one of the youngest and most notorious crime boss who ever lived. Many feared the racketeer, yet at the same time, idolized him.
The Ku Klux Klan marched in self appointed judge, jury, and executioner growing in a membership of 5 million in a relatively short period of time.
And The Great Depression tugged at many shirt tails with poverty, sickness, and suicide.

America was in the midst of its ever-changing ways, people were changing, styles were changing, even Moscow's Methodists were changing, but God's love remains constant. It was because of the Lords call to making disciples of all nations that the Moscow Methodist Men chose to build a new church, one that would accommodate the growing membership and the great need to continue in the service of God's call to love.

"Have you not known?
Have you not heard?
The everlasting God, the Lord,
The Creator of the ends of the earth,
Neither faints nor is weary.
His understanding is unsearchable."

Isaiah 40:28

Part III

Moscow Methodist Episcopal Church

"The Hand Dug Basement Church"

February 1930 – March 1954

Pastors who served Moscow "Hand Dug Basement Methodist Church
(Stevens County History Association, 1979)

1928–1930 - Frank Neff	1931-1937 - Karl Schuster
1938-1941 - Delbert Ester	1942-1944 - V.J. Ross
1945-1946 - Grace Gruising	1946 Spring – Roy Krause
1947 – Bob Brooks	1947-1950 – B.F. Young
1951 – W.H. Zook	1952-1953 – B.A. Scott

After 27 years, the people of Moscow found that they had outgrown the small structure. There were many fond memories in the little frame church, but the congregation was in need of a little more room to accommodate their service to God. So, in 1929, plans for a new, better equipped church building began.

Rev and Mrs. V.J. Ross
1942 -1944

1929 - 1930 saw many changes. **Hollywood** held its first ever Academy Awards. Two-hundred and fifty people attended the black tie event. Filet of Sole, Sauté au Buerre, and a half-broiled chicken on toast was served to the famous guests. Actor Emil Jannings won best actor for his portrayal in *'The Last Command: The Way of All Flesh'*.

October 29, 1929 became known as **Black Tuesday** and would go down in the history books as the day of the Great Stock Market Crash. The Great Depression brought an end to a long-standing celebration known as the 'Roaring Twenties'. This celebration came about during a time of great economic growth. Aristocrats and socialites became proletariats. Following the fall of the stock market, beautiful neighborhoods fell prey to the banks and Shanty-towns, more commonly known as Hoovervilles, popped up under bridges and in every vacant lot as the same aristocrats lost their financial prolificity. Extravagant Gatsby parties were replaced with soup kitchens, poverty, pain, and sickness. The gaiety of the Charleston, Tango, and the Shimmy were gone and dance marathons became a means of getting some money for the financially desperate.

> *"And He said to them, "Take heed and beware of covetousness,[a] for one's life does not consist in the abundance of the things he possesses."*
>   Luke 12:15

All meals were served with dish towels or other sorts of covering to prevent dust invading the sanctity of the meal, livestock died from their lungs becoming clogged with dirt and Dust Pneumonia, a form of pneumonia caused from breathing in the dust. This became a problem for people, as well. In the vain attempt to avoid the dust storm illness, people were covering their mouths and nose with wet handkerchiefs whenever they went outside, still many suffered and died. In April of 1935 Kansas alone had 17 deaths from Dust Pneumonia.

By March of 1930, 3.2 million Americans out of work in the United States alone (SoftSchools.com) With Kansas at the very heart, "The Dirty Thirties" engulfed 6 states including Texas, Oklahoma, Kansas, Nebraska, Colorado, and New Mexico (Venturio Media, LLP, 2012). The dust storms continue from 1930 to 1936 taking with it any hope of a healthy diet or income.

The world was changing, however, the little town of Moscow and their church continued to praise and serve the Lord. It continued Gods word to love one another even as he loved us..   (LJM)

When the decision was made to build a new church, the Moscow Methodist Episcopal men together with many volunteers began digging in an area that would become the new location of the better equipped Moscow Methodist Episcopal Church.

Even with the hardships and poverty, the ground-breaking service went on as scheduled and the construction began with whatever was available, shovels, spades, muscle, and sweat, all by volunteers and donations while the "Ladies Aid" worked tirelessly preparing the meals and beverages for the workers.

According to Mrs. Hazel Miller, the basement church was located on the northeast corner of Cook and Crawford across from the original parsonage and would become a source of pride and excitement. The women of the "Ladies Aid" were especially proud of the new church. "It has *two* restrooms and *three* classrooms." and the kitchen was "large enough to cook meals like the bigger churches. (Miller, 2013) The excitement was felt throughout the town! They "could now serve meals, hold bazaars, and do all sorts of things just like the big churches." (Stevens County History Association, 1979) And they did.

(right) An advertisement for a six cylinder Chevrolet that appeared in the Hugoton Hermes on May 2, 1930.

THE MOSCOW LADIES AID

A stranger came to Moscow one day;
This is what someone heard him say:
How do you ever keep your preacher paid?
Why, we can always rely on our Ladies Aid.

When we get back on our preacher's pay
The Ladies Aid put on a play.
And when the pocket book gets thinner and thinner,
The Ladies Aid have a chicken dinner.

 When they ask for donations from near and far,
You will know the Ladies Aid are planning a bazaar.
They have diminished teas, hobby fairs, doll shows –
How they get it all done, no one ever knows.

Fair weather or foul, it is all the same,
They serve ice cream at the punkin' gall game.
And if you want some good lemonade,
Just call on the Moscow Ladies Aid.

When they get tired of that, for a change, why then
They have a dinner served by the Moscow men.
They are indeed well-known far and wide –
Last year they painted the church inside.

Put a sink in the parsonage, fixed the preacher's well,
What they will do next, you never can tell;
You can count on the Aid for sure and certain,
They even helped pay for the brand-new curtain.

Now they have divided the Aid in four groups,
And are serving the public some excellent soups.
When do they do this, I hear you say –
They serve dinner and supper every Tuesday.

Their meats, beans, and coffee are all of the best,
You wonder when they ever find time to rest.
When husbands come home feeling tired and old,
Finds the kichen (sic) unswept, the house empty and cold,

The dishes unwashed, the beds unmade –
He will know his wife is helping the Ladies Aid.
Does he grumble and mutter and sit down and sigh?
No, he will put on his hat, to the church he will fly.

Be a sensible man, make no comments,
And get a good dinner for twenty-five cents.
Yes sir, grown-ups a quarter, children a dime,
Wish we could eat at the church all the time.

When dinner is over, he will feel happy and gay,
Tho' he is the one that has to pay, pay and pay.
When wife has been to a Ladies Aid meeting,
Husband is apt to be met with this kind of greeting:

"I think we will have a cold supper tonight,
For I have been out to Aid and cannot eat a bite,"
Their work for the future is not quite clear –
Except to paint the parsonage inside and out this year.

Mend the leaks in the parsonage roof,
Do many more things – if they have money enough.
So they all put on their aprons and are not afraid
To come out and work for the Ladies Aid.

Come work for the Aid, come one, come all –
United we stand, divided we fall.
Though the winds get high and the dust begins to roll
We will still serve soup in the old dust bowl.

As the man drove away, some one (sic) heard him say,
I wish I could have stayed
In a town where they have
Such a good Ladies Aid.

                                        -author unknown

This poem was written in recognition of The Ladies Aid. There is no date or author name, however it is very possible it was written sometime during the 1930's.

The planning and construction of the new church would not come easy. Timing would make this financially difficult, at the very least, however, the congregants would not be deterred. The members of this little church believed in God's blessings, and that He would provide.

"He is like a man building a house, who dug deep and laid the foundation on the rock. And when the flood arose, the stream beat vehemently against that house, and could not shake it, for it was founded on the rock." Luke 6:48

Money for the new building was earned anyway the members could think of. The Ladies Aid jumped into gear and began cooking meals for building supplies. They served a noontime meal to anyone who was able to pay a quarter and if they came back in the evening, they were served leftovers for a dime. The first bazaars provided between $40.00 and $50.00 which was very exciting, especially when you consider that a quart of milk cost 12¢ (49¢ a gallon) and a loaf of bread cost 7¢.

The bazaar which the ladies aid present annually will be on Thanksgiving Day this year to prevent a conflict with the high school play The noon meal will be served promptly at twelve so as not to interfere with afternoon plans. Supper will be served also at the church basement and a play will be given in the evening with the auction also several short numbers will be prsented of interest. Everyone is invited to be present and enjoy them selves, Nov. 28.

Bible study class will be on Wednesday evening of this week at seven at seven forty-five a choir practice Everyone is invited to take part in the practice and help have a lively Moscow continued choir.

"Members and friends of the church" pledged what they could, Sherwood Lumber Co. was the first to step up. The Moscow based company donated $200.00.

C.A. Kocher	$ 100.00	O.F. Jones	$ 5.00
A.R. Morrell	100.00	L.R. Joy	10.00
E.O. Brown	50.00	Bethel	5.00
H.C. Brown	50.00	J.T. Gray	10.00
H.E. Shuler	50.00	Robt. McGill	25.00
Frank Lahey	10.00	Leland Anderson	15.00
J.W. Ray	10.00	Anna Hartzell	5.00
J.H. Chaffin	....	Chas E Dudley	25.00
J.H. Cadman	10.00	Lon Gaskill	50.00
C.E. Bible	25.00	I.N. Shriver	100.00
C.A. Roland	25.00	Melvin Miller	25.00
A.J. Schmoock	25.00	F.H. Neff	50.00
Jim Cordry	2.00	Ralph Lowe	50.00
R. May	10.00	T.A. Dudley	50.00
W.C. Grandstaff	50.00	Eva Spurgeon	45.00
H. Myrick	20.00	A.B. Bromell	10.00
Glenn Hunsingeer	20.00	Elsie Hall	1.00
Walter Hunsinger	20.00	O.K. Pearse	15.00
Grant Shafford	5.00	R.L. Frazier	10.00
Chas Shafford	5.00	H.H. Wolfemeyer	15.00
H. Nordland	10.00	Herman Bromell	10.00
C.M. Graham	50.00	Arthur Lahey	50.00
Paul Wilson	20.00	J.E. (Ward?)	45.00
Milton Shriver	20.00	Emil Anderson	25.00
C.H. Bunton	....	Moscow State Bank	100.00
Ernest Roberson	15.00	W.A.T. Thomson	5.00
Geo. W Shaw	25.00	John O'Dea	15.00
Pearl Rhine	10.00	Doroty Harper	5.00
Intf and juniors			

Many people donated cash, others donated meals for the workers, or supplies such as concrete. When more donations were needed, the Ladies Aid went to work again, driving out to visit those in the country asking for contributions. People were very happy to donate what they could and if they had no money to give, that was okay, the Ladies were grateful for the fellowship and refreshment that they enjoyed during their visit.

As the construction continued, it became more and more obvious that the countries financial strife was going to hinder the efforts to building on the basement.

Hazel Miller said, they "only built the basement section because that was all they could afford so that was all they built." I guess God decided that was all we needed. (Miller, 2013)

The members did not mind worshiping in a basement, it was a wonderful basement, but there was one problem. Without the main floor, there was no belfry to hang that old bell? Then someone suggested that they would construct a special frame in front of the church and the bell could hang there. The others agreed thinking it was a wonderful solution to an otherwise difficult problem. That old bell would continue to ring calling all servants into Gods service.

In February of 1930 the members gathered for a farewell to the little frame church and together they walked to the new basement church for the first official service.

Mr. Burton purchased the little frame church and moved it to his land just outside of Moscow. Later it was struck by lightning and burned to the ground. The location of Mr. Burton's property now sports a bed and breakfast.

Hear my cry, O God;
Attend to my prayer.
2 From the end of the earth I will cry to You,
When my heart is overwhelmed;
Lead me to the rock that is higher than I.
3 For You have been a shelter for me,
A strong tower from the enemy.
4 I will abide in Your tabernacle forever;
I will trust in the shelter of Your wings.

Psalm 61:1-4

(Kansas Historical Society, 2014)

During the time of the Dust Bowl, The Garden City News reported the harsh truth. Decline in wheat crops, Farm credit collateral up in the air, midnight darkness shrouds southwest as grime rolls in, mixed snow and dust found in Goodland and Norton. Farmers were losing the battle for their crops and a boy and girl had been lost in a dirt storm. They were later found and said to be okay, unfortunately this was not always the case.

On one spring day, Hugoton had decided that it might be fun to have a countywide Easter Cantata. So when the Hugoton church invited Moscow, the invitation was accepted enthusiastically. The members of the Moscow Methodist Episcopal choir included: "Mary and Hilton Prather, Lucy Maxwell, Keith Roland" and Ida Shriver. (Stevens County History Association, 1979)

The first practice was held that Sunday at the Hugoton High School. The choir made their way to Hugoton then, shortly after practice began, the county sheriff came by and announced that there was a bad dust storm coming their way and advised everyone to go home without delay.

There did not seem to be time for thought. Everyone jumped into their automobiles and quickly headed home. The Moscow choir was only a few miles outside of town when they suddenly saw a large flock of birds as they flew over the automobile. When the five members looked in the direction the birds were flying from they were startled to see a thick black wall of dirt coming up fast. It was senseless to try and outrun the storm with the winds that blew about 60MPH while the auto could only go about 30MPH. The blowing top soil engulfed the Moscowites stalling the vehicle in a thick black cloud of dirt and dust. There was nothing they could do but cover their faces and crowd together.

Fear not, for I am with you;
Be not dismayed, for
I am your God.
I will strengthen you,
Yes, I will help you,
I will uphold you with My righteous right hand.'
Isaiah 41:10

The wind and blowing dirt was so strong that the choir was sure it would blow the car and them with it, right over.

Finally, after a few hours the wind and dirt did subside and they were able to make their way back to town. After that experience the idea of a countywide cantata was never brought up again.
(Hugoton Hermes, 1931)

Southwest Kansas was reportedly among the hardest hit areas during the Dust Bowl. Dust storms, such as the postcard above, rolled over the southern Great Plains between the years of 1932 and 1936. The storms removed top soil from the land which "prompting important changes in agricultural practice." It was discovered that if the farmers planted the same crop year after year essential nutrients important to keep the soil fertile would be depleted, thereby nothing would be able to grow. This was what happened and caused the now infamous 'dirty thirties'. Farmers were instructed to

rotate their crops so those nutrients one crop took would have a few years to replenish themselves. If, however, the agricultural community chose not to heed this advice, the Dust Bowl of the 1930's would not be the last.
(Kansas Historical Society, 2014)

The Ladies Aid spent a lot of time providing for the church and community, but they were not 'all work and no play'. In fact, many members could be found having, maybe a little too much fun, even despite what was going on around the country.

The Hugoton Hermes, dated November 20, 1931, published this poem in its Moscow News section.

"MORAL"
"We see a lad twist in and out,
Through traffic in the street,
Astride two wheels he noiselessly
Propels it with his feet.

We scowl and say he'll break his neck
The reckless little tike.
But wait "old man". Back up and think
You used to ride a bike.

"I call to mind the thrill I had,
When first I learned to ride.
the bumps and brusises (sic) soon forgot
When smoothly I could glide.

I conquered Newtons (sic) tricky law,
With balance, speed and skill
Small wonders that my joy was full
Who wouldn't get a thrill.

Why do we frown at childish pranks,
'Tis jealousy I we'en
If we would try those childish stunts to do,
We'd rather not be seen.

Don't laugh at Shriver or at Smith,
Because they like to ride
You'd like to do the stunt yourself
If you had some place to hide."
(Hugoton Hermes, 1931)

Further, into the same edition, an article appears which read:

"Milton Shriver borrowed Alvin Gaskill's bicycle and took a spin down the sidewalk, on west Main Street the other day. He took all the sidewalk and a part of the alley for right-of-way, but managed to keep right side up by letting his feet drag a little at times. Milton said that the bicycle didn't work like his old one at home did." (Hugoton Hermes, 1931)

The Ladies Aid

The Ladies of our little town
And from the country around,
Their work producing help and cheer,
are widly known far and near.
Their fame hereabouts is not a joke,
A corporation never broke,
When big church budgets must be paid
The preacher asks the Ladies Aid.

At Public sales the Ladies meet
To furnish all a bite to eat,
With steaming coffee, home made pies,
Hamburger steak and chicken fries.
A real square meal for every one.
Don't be afraid to spend the "mon"
It goes for good, each nickle paid,
When handed to the Ladies Aid.

At entertanment or bazaar,
A welcome guest you always are,
Do not be bashful, see the show,
The dough you spend will always go
To help the needy, help to send
The peace on earth good will to men
Through heavens gate our entrance make,
Again we meet the Ladies Aid

Milton Shriver was born John Milton Shriver and was the husband of Ida Shriver, who was a Moscow school teacher for some years. Mrs. Shriver taught the second and third grade and was a long time supporter and member of the Moscow Methodist Episcopal Church. When Mrs. Shriver passed away, the school dedicated their new gymnasium in her honor, the Ida Shriver Gymnasium.

" for I was hungry and you gave Me food;
I was thirsty and you gave Me drink;
I was a stranger and you took Me in"
Matthew 25:35

Moscow's Methodists have always taken the bible verse of Matthew 25:35, very serious.

The article to the right demonstrates this mission oriented church very well when it says "Not what we do for ourselves but for others, bring us real joy" (Hugoton Hermes, 1931)

> Mr. Ward and Mr. Schuster worked Monday on the screens for the church which will divide the young peoples Sunday school class from the Bible class. This will be welcomed by all.
>
> Church Calendar:
> Sunday school 10:00 a. m.
> Morning worship, 11:00 a. m.
> Epworth League, 6:30 p. m.
> Evening worship, 7:15, p. m.
> Next Sunday is promotion day in the Sunday school. Attendance in Sunday school has been increasing. Will you not come next Sunday and help us reach a goal of one hundred twenty-five.
> Next Sunday is also Missionary Sunday, the ideal toward which we strive is to have every member of the Sunday school and church give to missions. Not what we do for ourselves but for others, bring us real joy.

Purportedly the image to the left was the first one room school house in Moscow. It was donated to the Stevens County Gas and Historic Museum by the City of Moscow and is on display at the museum.

This would put the building on the North end of Main Street in the first block.

In 1950 the Ladies Aid took on a fundraiser that included publishing a Church cookbook. The book included many recipes from the members of the church including; Mush biscuits by Mrs. H.E. McCue and Mrs. B.R. Young's recipe for Orange-nut bread.

There are many cooking tips, such as how to measure 1/2 teaspoon from a teaspoon, something we may be able to do rather easily if you are math savvy, or by simply using our 'handy-dandy" 1/2 teaspoon from your set of measuring spoons. Mrs. J.E. Ward was in charge of advertising, along with Mrs. Glen Gaskill. Recipe Collection was Mrs. Milton Shriver and Mrs. Glen Gaskill. Final recipe selection was the responsibility of Mrs. Henry Nichols, Mrs. Alvin Gaskill and Mrs. M.M. McCue.

The ladies also included a couple of "Sayings":

Advice to the thin: don't eat fast *Advice to the fat; don't eat fast*	*In all ranks of life the human heart yearns for the beautiful; and the beautiful things that God makes are his gift to all alike. (Stowe)*

Also included with this cookbook was a dedication to one of their own who had passed on:

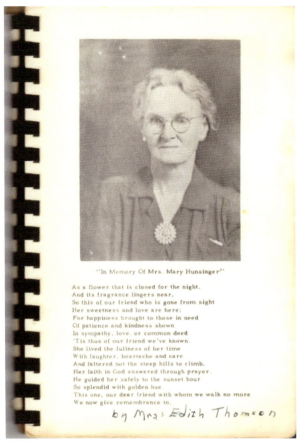

"In Memory Of Mrs. Mary Hunsinger"

As a flower that is closed for the night.
And its fragrance lingers near.
So this of our friend who is gone from sight
Her sweetness and love are here;
For happiness brought to those in need
Of patience and kindness shown
In sympathy, love, or common deed
'Tis thus of our friend we've known.
She lived the fullness of her time
With laughter, heartache and care
And faltered not the steep hills to climb,
Her faith in God answered through prayer.
He guided her safely to the sunset hour
So splendid with golden hue.
This one, our dear friend with whom we walk no more
We now give remembrance to.
        by Mrs. Edith Thomson

There were many hardships during the thirties. More than the deaths of loved ones or others we shared our lives with for a time. There were the dirt storms of the Dust Bowl, and the Depression, topping the list. But, according to more than one source: Even the notorious Barrow gang, with Bonny and Clyde spent some time in Hugoton hiding out until, that is, the city sheriff Charles H. Newman was killed by Fred McBee on October 12, 1931. Even though Bonny and Clyde had not shot the sheriff, with all the attention on Hugoton, they had decided it was time to go.

Hugoton Stevens County, Kansas, Friday, October 30, 1931

FRED McBEE BEING TRIED FOR MURDER OF C. H. NEWMAN

Large Crowds Throng the Court Room and Grounds As the Trial Progresses. Many Jurors Are Rejected In Effort To Select the Necessary Twelve.

BULLETIN—As we go to press the jury has not been chosen in the case of State vs. McBee, charged with the murder of City Marshal C. H. Newman. The state has made one peremptory challenge and the defense two. Each time a challenge is made it means that several more men will be examined before another juror is tentatively chosen. The jury may be finally selected this Thursday afternoon, and then it may take until Friday.

The Hermes will carry a full account of the murder and the trial next week.

The trial of Fred McBee, accused of the murder of C. H. Newman, city marshal, of Hugoton, was called for trial on Wednesday of this week.

The defendant was brought into court where he, through his attorneys, W. E. Eddy of Hugoton and G. W. Sawyer of Liberal, waived formal ar-

in The Hermes and other papers published in southwest Kansas. Some of the questions asked indicated that the defense considered it a ground for disqualifying a juryman because he could read and had read accounts of the killing in the papers. It also carried with it the insinuation that a great wrong had been committed by The Hermes and other newspapers in saying anything about the case at all and that a still greater wrong had been done the defendant by newspapers or any one else suggesting that the conditions leading up to the murder and which were the direct cause of the killing should be rectified.

Ed. Jones' name was brought into the case during the examination of the jurors. Mr. Jones is a former sheriff of this county and a personal friend of the dead marshal. The jurors were also closely questioned as to whether they had been approached by any organization and asked to sign any petition asking for a clear

(Hugoton Hermes, 1931)

Bonny and Clyde were known in Hugoton as Blackie and Jewel. Clyde, aka "Blackie", worked outside of Hugoton while Bonny aka "Jewel", ran a café in town. Another source says that Bonny played house wife in a small house between Hugoton and Moscow, on a farm in which Clyde worked. Purportedly, she got bored of the hum-drum life style and influenced Clyde through complaints to leave the job.

Another story tells us that there was an argument on Main Street in Hugoton between 'Blackie' and one of his cronies. 'Blackie' was stabbed and left for dead. An onlooker went to his aid until someone from the hospital could come and take care of Clyde. The onlooker was a woman who knew medicine and knew exactly who she was keeping alive while word got to Liberal and the hospital came. Clyde Barrow most assuredly would have died in those three hours it took to get a doctor back to town. (anonymous) Yet another source said that Bonnie and Clyde stayed at a Bed and Breakfast outside of Hugoton. Interestingly enough, I ran into a want ad that was advertised in the Hugoton Hermes archives for a man and wife who would work outside of town and live in a small house between Hugoton and Moscow a couple of weeks after Bonnie and Clyde supposedly left town.

It is up to you as to what you want to believe. As for me, I think they did a good job of keeping us guessing.

Many difficult situations had been worked through, with God's blessings guiding the members, however, they were not all difficult circumstances or tough decisions. One specific decision that was made brought a kindergarten class to town of Moscow. The town school did not have a kindergarten class and was not able to offer one due to a variety of reasons including financial. But God must have felt one was necessary.

Mrs. Thomson, who was a school teacher by trade, came to the church and asked permission to use the basement. She wanted to use the church weekdays, 'just' in the mornings to teach the children kindergarten. She was extremely unwavering in her belief that kindergarten was essential to a child's education. The church, seeing this as a good opportunity for Moscow's children and a wonderful way to continue with God's work gave Mrs. Thomson their blessings. From that time on the church served as a school for five year olds during the week and for Sunday school and worship on Sundays.

> *"But Jesus said, "Let the little children come to Me and do not forbid them; for of such is the kingdom of heaven."*
> Matthew 19:14

And the old bell rang on...

*"For He established a testimony in Jacob,
And appointed a law in Israel,
Which He commanded our fathers,
That they should make them known to their children;
That the generation to come might know them,
The children who would be born,
That they may arise and declare them to their children,
That they may set their hope in God,
And not forget the works of God,
But keep His commandments;"*
 Psalm 78:57

Part IV

Moscow United Methodist Church

"The Brick Church"

March 1954 – November 2013

The end of the 1st hundred years and the beginning of another generation

Pastors who served Moscow "Brick" Methodist Church
(Stevens County History Association, 1979)

1953 – 1964 – C. Schweitzer	1964 – 1966 – Robert Ritter
1966 – 1971 – Gary Reynolds	1971 – 1972 – James Mardock
1972 – 1978 – Hugh Bishop	1978 – 1984 – Glenn Fogo
1984 – 1986 – Roger Thomas	1986 – 1987 – Loren Chapman
1987 – 1996 – David Randall	1996 – 1999 – R. Zimmerman
1999 – 2001 – Josué P. Mora	2001 – 2004 – William Ripley
2004 – 2006 – Roy Nelson	2006 – Present – Timothy McCrary

Moscow's first Methodist church, "the Little Frame Church" was located down what was then known as Main Street, today it is Cook Street. The second building, the "Hand Dug Basement Church", was located on the corner of, what is known today as Crawford Street and Cook Street.

Now, the Moscow's Methodists has grown so much, it had become necessary for yet another church building to be constructed. A larger church with more kitchen space to accommodate the people, a larger sanctuary, and maybe an office for the pastor. The basement church would have served well with another floor built on however, with the

BREAK GROUND FOR CHURCH Participants in ground-breaking ceremonies for the new Moscow Methodist Church on which construction work will begin immediately were, left to right: Rev Ben White, Bloom; Rev F E Rohl, Hugoton, Rev Delbert Ester, Sublette; Rev Bervie Scott, Moscow, A E Buck, architect, Boyd E Stehwein, contractor for the new building, and Walter Hunsinger, J E Ward, J L Brownell, Carl White, R V McCue and Jay Shriver, all on the church building committee Mr Brownell turned over the first spadeful of dirt during the ground-breaking ceremonies, attended by about 100 persons

Great Depression behind them and the land producing crops again, a bigger, more beautiful, new church was within their grasp. The decision to build was agreed on with enthusiastic cheers and excitement.

The ground-breaking ceremony was held on May 17, 1953. Participants, according to the Hugoton Hermes, included "left to right: Rev. Ben White, Bloom; Rev F. E. Rohl, Hugoton; Rev Delbert Ester, Sublette; Rev Bervie Scott, Moscow; A. E. Buck, architect, Boyd E. Stehwein, contractor for the new building, and Walter Hunsinger, J. C. Ward, J. L. Brownell, Carl White, R. V. McCue and Joy Shriver, all on the church building committee. Mrs. Brownell turned over the first spade full of dirt during ground-breaking ceremonies, attended by about 100 persons." (Hugoton Hermes, 1953)

It would be a beautiful church with a tall steeple in which to place that old bell that first rang the town to services in 1913.

It took close to a year to complete and many, many hours of fund raising to get the money to complete the construction. In 1913, the 'little frame church' cost a $1,800.00, a hefty amount back then. However, fifty years later, the 'new church' would cost $96,000 and an additional $53,000 only thirteen years later for a fellowship hall to be added.

WHAT A DIFFERENCE FIFTY YEARS MAKE

1881

Fifty years ago women wore hoopskirts, bustles, petticoats, corsets, cotton stockings, high buttoned shoes, ruffled cotton drawers, flannel nightgowns, puffs in their hair—did their own cooking, baking, cleaning, washing, ironing—raised big families—went to church Sunday—were too busy to be sick.

Men wore whiskers, square hats, Ascot ties, red flannel underwear, big watches and chains, chopped wood for stoves—bathed once a week, drank ten-cent whiskey and five cent beer—rode bicycles, buggies or sleighs—went in for politics—worked 12 hours a day, and lived to a ripe old age.

Stores burned coal oil lamps—carried everything from a needle to a plow—trusted everybody—never took an inventory—placed orders for goods a year in advance—always made money.

1931

Today women wear silk stockings, short skirts, low shoes, no corsets, an ounce of underwear, have bobbed hair, smoke, paint and powder, drink cocktails, play bridge, drive cars, have pet dogs, and go in for politics and petting.

Men have high blood pressure, wear no hats, and some no hair, shave their whiskers, shoot golf, bathe twice a day, drink poison, play the stock market, ride in airplanes—never go to bed the same day they get up—are misunderstood at home—work five hours a day, play ten—die young.

Stores have electric lights, cash registers, elevators, never have what the customer wants—trust nobody, take daily inventory—never buy in advance—have overhead-mark-up-down-quota-budget-advertising-stock control-annual and semi-annual, end-of-month, dollar day, founder's day, rummage, economy day sales—and never make any money.

Stanley McGill remembers as a young boy that the men would go to the bridge between Satanta and Moscow to get the sand to mix the cement for the church foundation. Mr. McGill said "All the concrete you see around the church was made from the sand that was carried up from under that bridge." He said he remembered that it was okay going down but it was a lot of huffing and puffing coming back up. (McGill, 2014)

Mr. McGill also tells a story of the Reverend Schweitzer, the first pastor at the new church. Mr. McGill said that Reverend Schweitzer who was a shorter man, one day picked up a sledgehammer (most likely about 15 lbs.) by the very end of the handle and held it straight up with his arm extended perpendicular to his body.

(An original bulletin was found in the basement of the new brick church. This is an image of that first order of service March 21, 1954.)

```
THIS IS A COPY OF THE FIRST SERVICE HELD
IN THIS BUILDING.
=========================================

              MOSCOW METHODIST CHURCH
             Charles Schweitzer, Pastor
                  March 21, 1954
=========================================

Sunday School Worship              10:00 A. M.
Mrs. Ida Shriver     Sunday School Superintendent
Lesson:  What is the New Commandment?
Memory Verse:  A new commandment I give you,
that you love one another; even as I have loved
you, that you love one another.    John 13:34
=========================================

MORNING WORSHIP                    11:00 A. M.

Prelude          the people in devout meditation

CALL TO WORSHIP                    Choir - #589

HYMN                               #396

RESPONSIVE READING    The Blessed Life    #573

GLORIA PATRI

SCRIPTURE READING

PRAYER                       Choral Response

OFFERING

SPECIAL                        Lillie Miller

SERMON                           Communion

HYMN                               #149

BENEDICTION

POSTLUDE                            Pianist
As the heart panteth after the water brooks, so

panteth my soul after thee, O God.  Psalm 42:1
```

The Reverend then tipped the hammer end down and touched his nose with it before raising it up again! He may have been small, but that man was strong! (McGill, 2014)

A task with many hands makes light that task. The members of the congregation did quite a bit of the work, at least what they could do. The work they could not do was done by construction workers. So the women cooked, the men worked, all were feed, and finally, finally the bell was hung.

The final service at the basement church was on March 21, 1954. It had been five months from laying the cornerstone and nine months from the ground-breaking ceremony before the new church was ready to move into. So on March 21 of that year, the congregation met at the basement church, held the first half of their service and then together walked the two blocks to their new house of worship. The service began with Lillie Miller, accompanied by Wayne Comer singing "Bless this House". Lillie Miller had sung the first song in all three building.

The first wedding was on May 23, 1954 uniting Marilyn Sue McClure and Gary Eugene Brewer. On April 18, 1954, James Craig Kapp, Rhonda Kay Christian, Beth Ann Henrickson, Carol Sue LaForce, and Sheri Ellen Teeter were the first babies to be baptized in the new brick church and a boy scout troop meet at the church. A troop of boys that would bring pride to the town of Moscow and the congregation of the Moscow Methodist Church.

On April 17, 1955, the boys in troop 187 were awarded a great honor, the God and Country Award.

The Reverend Schweitzer (1953-1964) had the great honor of presenting the troop with the award. It is a tremendous achievement for the scouts and a proud moment for everyone.

BOY SCOUT BADGES

Moscow hosted a Girl Scout troop for a time; however, it was relatively short lived due to the lack of interest among the young ladies.

This typewritten article was sent to the church pastor by Mrs. Hazel McCue along with some other records of Ralph McCue's. There is no author name with the only date mentioned in the article as being October of 1974, however it gives an inspiring account of:

Scouting in Moscow

Shortly after the completion of the new Methodist Church in Moscow, sixteen Boy Scouts were given the God and Country Award on April 17, 1955. Rev. Chas. Sweitzer worked very hard in this achievement. Kenneth Hendrickson was Scoutmaster and Chet LaForce was his assistant, with Ralph McCue always helping. The boys receiving the award were Clovis Brewer, Ronald Brewer, Roy Bundy, Ray Curtis, Roy Curtis, George Hall, Roger Hall, Richard Hirn, Darrel Miller, Lynn Miller, Terry Miller, Dennis Pearce, Lynn Seabolt, Jack Stoddard, Carl Thurow and Arthur Tilford. As far as we know, this is the largest group of scouts receiving this coveted award at one time from the same troop in our whole United States.

Scouting was organized in Moscow, Kansas in about the year 1938. At the time, 19 southwest counties were placed in a new council called Santa Fe Trail Council. The first president of the new council was A.E. "Gus" Kramer of Hugoton, followed later by Ralph McCue and Robert Fox of Moscow, all three of whom hold the award of "Silver Beaver."

Even before this time Dr. O.K. Pearce, a local veterinarian often took the boys around town on excursions in the area looking for arrowheads, rocks and fossils. The group was often referred to as Dr. Pearce and his Scouts although they were not organized at the time. Ralph McCue took the guiding hand when Boy Scouts were organized.

A Tribute to Ralph McCue and His Wife, Hazel.

Santa Fe Trail Council is great because of the work done in scouting by people like Ralph and Hazel McCue. They have given many years of cheerful service to their community, their church, and to western Kansas.

With no children of their own, Ralph has served as Scoutmaster, committee member, and Institutional representative of Troop 187 of Moscow. He has been continually active for more than 30 years. Serving two terms as Council President. He is a holder of the Silver Beaver Award, the top council honor in scouting.

The McCues, besides making heavy contributions in time and money toward the purchase and development of the Spanish Peaks Scout Ranch (purchased while Ralph was president of the council). (Hazel McCue loaned to the Council a substantial sum ot a low interest rate) so that the purchase and development could be completed).

Scouts and Scouters for many years to come will enjoy camping in the Rocky Mountains because Ralph and Hazel McCue had the vision, faith and inspiration to invest in the future. By their leadership, we have one of the finest camps in America. (Mr. McCue died in October, 1974 as this tribute was being given in the Santa Fe Trail Echo.

The Methodist Church continues the sponsorship of the Troop 187 and the community is improved by an active scouting program. (Unknown, Scouting In Moscow, 1974)

The "Silver Beaver" is an award presented to "registered Scouters of exceptional character who have provided distinguished service within a council" (Silver Beaver Award, 2014) It is for registered leaders who have made a significant impact on the youth under their direction through community service.

Dr. Pearce's arrowhead collection is on display at the Stevens County Gas and Historical Museum and many of the arrowheads included in his collection are those the scouts found with Dr. Pearce.

Burial Services Last Sunday for Martha Reynolds

Mrs. W R Reynolds, age 83, Moscow resident since 1898, died February 1, in the Stevens County Hospital where she had been receiving treatment for three weeks for a critical illness.

Funeral services were conducted in the Moscow Metho-

Martha L. Reynolds

dist Church, Sunday, February 4, at 2:30 p.m. and burial was in Moscow cemetery in the family lot.

Rogers of Hugoton was in charge of arrangements. A time from 2:00 to 8:00 p.m. Saturday was arranged for friends to call at the Rogers chapel in Hugoton, and from 10:30 a.m., until time of services at her home in Moscow.

George Ferguson, soloist sang two hymns, "Rock of Ages" and "In the Garden."

Survivors included relatives of Moscow, Denver, Colo., and Rockport, Mo. She had no immediate relatives.

Martha Reynolds, a long time Moscowite, moved to Stevens County by covered wagon, four years after her mother passed away. She married Walter (Jud) Reynolds in 1898 at the age of twenty and in 1913 they came with the rest of the town to its present location.

Mr. Reynolds was the Moscow Bank president and had built a beautiful three bedroom home on Ransom Street. Mr. Reynolds passed away in 1942. Mrs. Reynolds lived until she was 83 years old.

With no immediate family to leave her home to, she did the next best thing; she left it to the church. Mrs. Reynolds, herself was not a woman known to be a strong Christian. She never attended the Methodist Church

claiming ties to the Lutheran denomination of which she was raised in. Still, she left her home to the church.

Mrs. Martha Reynolds' home would become the new parsonage and Reverend Schweitzer, the first to move in. Such a wonderful gift to the Moscow United Methodist Church family. Since its original construction, many upgrades have been made, however, the beauty of the home with its oval archways, stained woodworking and baseboards still remain.

During the Christmas holidays, the home was once said to look like "a gingerbread house."

The Parsonage and the Pear tree

The article pictured was first published in the Hugoton Hermes following Mrs. Reynolds death in February of 1962.

The house was dedicated to the ministry and blessed in the sight of the congregation.

In October 29, 1972, ten years later in 1972, the congregation would celebrate yet another dedication service. In this celebration, the beautiful stained glass windows were blessed. You may believe that the stained glass windows are simply various symbols of the Christian faith and you would be partially correct, however, according to the 1973 church directory, each window is an iconic representation of one disciple of Jesus Christ. Each window was paid for by members of the congregation and dedicated in the memory of a loved one.

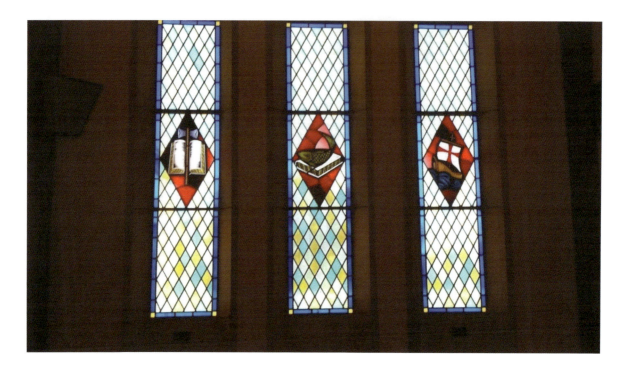

MATTHIAS (replaced Judas)
Open Bible with an ax:
Preached in Syria. Died by being beheaded, Another account says he was burned to death.
Martyred: 70 A.D
In memory of Clyde Bunton
By wife Helen

SIMON the ZEALOT
A Fish:
Simon the Zealot ministered in Persia. He was killed because he refused to sacrifice to the sun god.
Martyred: 74 A.D
In memory of Mr. & Mrs. H.E. McCue and Leland Anderson
By Donna Anderson

JUDE (Thaddeus) *A Boat with a Maltese shaped cross:*
Traveled far on missionaries with Simon. Said to have been beaten to death by sticks.
Martyred: 72 A.D
In memory of sister Nellie Mae Koeford by Ross and Beryl

JAMES THE LESSER
Hand Saw:
Said to have been "sawn asunder" after a horrible martyrdom. Another account says he was poisoned and then cast down from the temple and beaten to death for not denying Jesus' resurrection.
Martyred: 63 A.D.
In memory of George W. Shaw and Alberta Shaw by Nettie Shaw and Woodrow Shaw

PHILIP
A cross and two loaves of bread:
Ministry in Carthage, North Africa and Asia Minor. Said to have died cruelly in retaliation of converting the Roman proconsul's wife.
Martyred: 54 A.D
In memory of   Roxanne Cooper By Archie Cooper, Margaret Cooper, Myron and Marlin

ANDREW
Anchor with cross:
Brought the gospel to Soviet Union and preached in Asia Minor, Turkey and Greece. Crucified.
Martyred: 70 A.D
By Bob and Laura McGill.

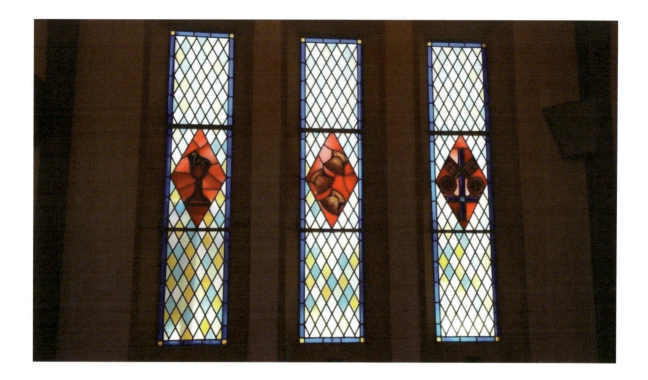

JOHN
Chalice with the snake:
Jesus told John, from the cross, to take care of His mother. He is said to have drank poison from a chalice and lived. Also said to have been cast into boiling oil and not hurt.
Lived to old age and died of natural causes.
Martyred: 95 A.D
In memory of Bertha Ward, by Hazel Miller

JAMES THE GRATER
Three shells:
Martyred by sword at the order of Herod Agrippa. The executioner is said to have witnessed the courage and unrelenting spirit of James, come to believe in the resurrection and then he was also executed.
Martyred: 44-45 A.D
In memory of Bertha Ward. by Hazel Miller

PETER
An upside down cross
Said to have been martyred by crucifixion in Rome in about 66 A.D. upside down. He felt unworthy to die in the same way Jesus did.
In memory of J.L Brownell by Mae Brownell, Muriel Frisbie, Miriam Wainman, Mary Smith

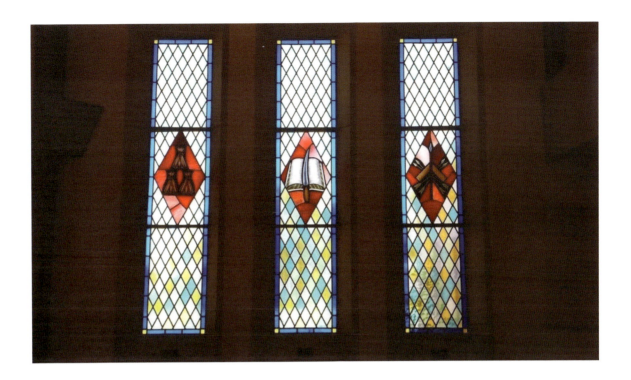

MATTHEW
Three stacks of wheat:
Ministered in Persia and Ethiopia. Some accounts say he lived to old age, others say he was stabbed to death.
Martyred: 60-70 A.D.
In memory of Helen McGill Thurow by Ralph and Carl Mac Thurow

BARTHOLOMEW
An open bible with a knife:
Missions in India, Armenia, Ethiopia, and south Arabia. Martyrdom. Not known how.
Martyred: 70 A.D.
In memory of Maurice M. McCue by Blanche McCue – Janice Sheffield

"DOUBTING" THOMAS
A carpenter's square and a spear:
Active in Syria, preached in India. Died by spear.
Martyred: 70A.D.
In memory of Mr. & Mrs. John Chaffin by the Chaffin children: Owen, Leona, Bill, Gary, Paul, Zoeme, Jr. Chaffin

The three liturgical tower shaped windows behind the alter represent:

THE FATHER – The hand surrounded by the _cruciform nimbus_ *
In memory of Maurice McCue by Blanche McCue and Dick McCue

THE SON – the lamb with unfolding banner and cruciform nimbus. In memory of Maurice M McCue by Blanche McCue and Larry McCue

THE HOLY SPIRIT – the dove with the cruciform nimbus
In tribute to Will and Nora Christian by their children; Wilda Haggard, Bernice Bradley, Cathryn Jantz, Mary Hall, Willis Christian, Everett Christian
I AM THE WAY, THE TRUTH, AND THE LIFE – In memory of Everett Shuler by Chrystal, his wife.
(MUMC, 1973) (Unknown, Dedication of Stained Glass Windows) (Patton, 2014) (Ken Curtis, 2014)
* (A _cruciform nimbus_ is the iconic halo with the cross shown behind Jesus' head.)

This photo was taken May 11, 2014 after the Mothers Day service. It was the 100th anniversary of celebrating mom's all over.

"Look at the birds of the air,
for they neither sow nor reap nor gather into barns;
yet your heavenly Father feeds them.
Are you not of more value than they?"
Matthew 6:26

There was a significant number of members who attended all three church buildings and in 1973, those who were still living had their picture taken together in the brick church. Hazel Miller was able to name most of them, with only a few names she could not recall.

Leslie Wolfemeyer, Ralph McCue, Laura McGill, Blanche McCue, Bob McGill, Mrs. Gaskill, Alvin Gaskill, Mrs. Thomson, Hazel McCue, Jay and Linda Shriver, Hazel and Roy Miller, Ray and Lillie Miller.

As of April 13, 2014, Mrs. Hazel Miller is the only surviving member who attended all three church buildings. According to Mrs. Miller, her parents, Jess and Bertha Ward became members of the church at a revival. In 1915, Mr. and Mrs. Ward had their little Hazel baptized in that "Little Frame Church". (Miller, 2013)

Many times you hear how little towns are so boring and there is simply nothing to do and never any excitement. Oh, contraire…

The 1980 Summer Olympics announced that they would be held in Russia. At that time, the United States had not been on very good terms with Russia. When the Soviet Russia invaded Afghanistan in 1979. President Carter "was eager to boycott the Moscow

Summer Olympics". He (President Carter) even enlisted the services of wrestler turned religious leader, Muhammad Ali as "an emissary to African nations to elicit their support for a boycott." U.S. officials were sent to Muhammad Ali who was in India at the time, to see if he would take the job. It was a total disaster with Muhammad Ali accused of being President Carter's 'puppet'. Still the U.S. government continued to push the boycott.

According to William Bigelow, the author of the Global Research article, 55% of Americans were in favor of the boycott, even though, the Olympians were not. (Bigelow, 2014)

With all of this going on in Washington and around

the world, little Moscow, Kansas had an idea that could solve all of the problems between the Soviet Russia and the White house. HOLD THE OLYMPICS IN MOSCOW (KANSAS). And it took off.

Who would have thought a joke that was started at a small café in a town of 250 inhabitants could become such an attraction that it would gain national attention. But it did!

No one knew just how far the people of Moscow (Kansas, that is) would let it go, but soon T-shirts and bumper stickers were created that read "Move the Olympics to Moscow, Kansas" letters were mailed to Johnny Carson and Paul Harvey, two celebrities with major followings.

According to the Hugoton Hermes in the April 3, 1980 edition, the "movement is rumored to have had its birth in Rosie's Diner."

1980's Summer Olympics, (staff, 2014) Moscow (Russia)

Moscow Russia *did not* have anything on Moscow, Kansas, though! Moscow had all of the facilities that Russia did! Rosie Lang, owner of Rosie's Café, said that the town's cesspool would make for a great swimming pool, transportation would be courtesy of the *greyhounds* (dog's from a local farm), the corn patches would make for adequate privacy, and a pay phone has already been okayed by the phone company. "Ya cain't ask for any thin' else, now could ya'?" Television crews can cover the events from the water tower (they git first dibs) but it will also make a great place for those who come to watch the events. "But, we'll also have to nail them down," said Rosie, "to keep them from blowing away, the wind blows so hare."

"Rounding out the city's qualifications as an alternate Olympic site is an airport, usually described as a "tin shed affair," two service stations, a building that houses the city hall, a boarded-up hotel, and a feed store."

Architect's drawing of the church before it was constructed
Drawing hangs in the Fellowship Hall.

Well, President Carter thought the town was joking but that did not stop the folks of Moscow! No, ma'am! Moscow held their *own* Olympic games that year. Jim Shaddix, proudly ran the 'zippo' torch all the way down Main Street, proudly raised high for the official lighting of the Moscow Olympics flame! Even the local news followed the antics.

The fun reached all the way to the White House with Vice-president Walter Mondale ordering three T-shirts, one for himself, one for the president, and another for Amy, the president's daughter. Of course, this was all in fun and was said to relieve tension that was created by Jimmy Carters call for a boycott.

"Nothing is better for a man than that he should eat and drink, and that his soul should enjoy good in his labor.
Ecclesiastes 2:24

Notes worth Noting

The life of a church is dependent on the faith of its members. If the members become lost like the sheep that follow their nose as he eats from the fragrant grass, then the church can becomes lost as well. Life can and often does get in the way of our faith, school, jobs, money and relationships, they all play a part in pulling us away like the fragrant grass pulls the absent minded sheep from its master. Our lives are in constant change. In every state you can hear someone say; "you don't like the weather, wait 5 minutes…" Everything changes, life changes, we change, the world around us is in a state of constant change! And through this change it can be easy to become lost. Lost in our own life changes or lost in the very things that should help to increase our faith.

Christmas is a perfect example of this. When we get so busy decorating, baking, entertaining, shopping, and any other preparation we have for the holiday, we can find that the reason we celebrate is gone, forgotten, or even Lost.

"Now it happened as they went that He entered a certain village; and a certain woman named Martha welcomed Him into her house. And she had a sister called Mary, who also sat at Jesus' feet and heard His word. But Martha was distracted with much serving, and she approached Him and said, "Lord, do You not care that my sister has left me to serve alone? Therefore tell her to help me."
And Jesus answered and said to her, "Martha, Martha, you are worried and troubled about many things. But one thing is needed, and Mary has chosen that good part, which will not be taken away from her."
Luke 10:38-42

What Martha was doing was very important. It would be rude to not take care of their guest's material needs. However, Mary was also doing what was important. Moscow church not only does the work that is essential to serve the Lord, but they also sit with the Lord similar to the way Martha sat with Jesus.

Rev Hugh Bishop
1972 - 1978

Moscow Methodist not only take care of the essential material needs, they continued to feed their spiritual needs, by trusting in the Lords grace and in his promises, by not letting life move them away from the Lord and their faith. By remembering to not only complete the work that needs to be done but to take the time to be with Him, as well.

What good is it if we take care of the material aspect of our lives without remembering exactly who is responsible for the essential material needs. When the children of Israel cried to Moses that they were going to die of thirst, it was the Lord who brought water from the rock! When Daniel was thrown into the lion's den, it was the Lord that kept the hungry lions away. The Lord is who makes everything possible. We would not have the material without the Lords blessings. We would not have life without Him.

Our physical needs are important, our spiritual needs are essential.

Thank you Father, for your blessings, we look to serve you in this life and in our forever life with you. Amen

In 1988, the Moscow United Methodist Church welcomed a sister church, The Moscow Baptist Church. The two denominations would come together in joint worship services, activities, and fundraisers. The charter minister Larry Bradford and Pastor Tim McCrary would become friends in service and ministry.

Some of the combined activities would be a golf tournament that is open to anyone. Rain or shine, the tournament would go on as planned.

In one tournament a much welcomed rain did come. Questions ran whether the tournament would be canceled or rescheduled. What would be the decision?

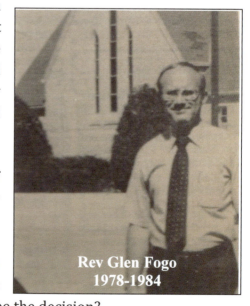

Rev Glen Fogo
1978-1984

The decision was made to not cancel, after all how long could it rain? This is southwest Kansas! The Lord loves a good laugh and He more than likely had a good one with this tournament because the rain poured in buckets but the tournament went on as scheduled. Everyone had a soaking good time.

The following is a page out of the 1988 combined church directory of the United Methodist Church and the Moscow Baptist Church. The directory was set up 'topsy turvey' style. You could go through the pages of one church, then to see the other church

Our History

Moscow Baptist Church is affiliated with the Southern Baptist Convention, the Kansas-Nebraska Convention of Southern Baptists, The Western Kansas Baptist Association, and the Stevens County Ministerial Association.

The church began as a mission project of Trinity Baptist Church of Hugoton, Kansas, in October, 1988. The first organizational meeting occurred at the Moscow Senior Center with subsequent worship services begin conducted at the Moscow Recreation Building. Rev. Larry Bradford, pastor of Trinity Baptist Church, also became the dual pastor of the Mission, holding worship services in Moscow at 9:00 a.m. and then returning to Hugoton to preach worship services at Trinity at 10:45 a.m.

July 1990

In February, 1990, with only 5 official church members and many supporters, the congregation voted to construct a church building. A volunteer work crew arrived and in the week following July 4th, 1990, the crew, along with many Mission attendees and Trinity members, constructed the first building in just 5 days. Inside and finishing work was completed in the months that followed by Mission members and volunteers.

Moscow Baptist Mission petitioned the SBC, KNCSB, and WKBA for full church status and Rev. Bradford became the full-time pastor January 1, 1997. Moscow Baptist Church constructed additional fellowship, storage and classroom space in the spring of 1999 and is currently debt-free with a membership of over 100.

you had to turn the directory upside down. This page was on the Baptist' side and describes their start in Moscow.

To bring another denomination into the town of Moscow was a welcome sight; it meant that the town was flourishing!

Many times different denominations do not see eye to eye. Beliefs differ slightly, but enough to cause a riff in the relationship. However, the differing beliefs did not do as much damage as it could have to the Moscowites. As a matter of fact, it actually helped the community!

In all of Gods wisdom, being that what it is, the two denominations brought more people into worship. Some folks might not have felt comfortable in the style of worship the United Methodist had and by opening the doors to another denomination, the important basics were still there, but the style of worship changed enough to welcome others into the Lords grace.

The Lord's blessings did not stop there. God brought the two denominations together for many reasons, helping in times of need, shared celebrations, and Fifth Sunday Sings. Fifth Sunday Sings brought community comradery and helped to remind the two they were united in Christ as one.

Many Fifth Sunday Sings would be celebrated with the newly found Baptist Hillbilly Band. The band would eventually go on to bring song and worship to various towns, communities, churches, and fairs. The band features a couple of guitars, a banjo, a fiddle, a mandolin, a Jews Harp, and even a gut-bucket! All dressed in over-alls and straw hats, the Baptist Hillbilly Band became a popular draw. What a wonderful way to celebrate the blessings of Christ.

.

A Letter from Pastor Josué Mora (1999 – 2001)

November 4, 2013

Dear Pastor Tim,

I still feel extremely awful for not being able to go to the 100th church anniversary in Moscow. On Thursday morning, October 31st we had our luggage already in the car when suddenly my wife began to feel sick, beside the terrible headaches that most of the time she has. Her diabetes has taken its toll. She can hardly walk, even with her walker. She gets tired very easily and probably she will not be able to travel any more. I did call you to let you know about it but I could not get thru, so I left the message in the church. With all of these worries I forgot to e-mail you.

If it is not too late and you would be kind enough to read this letter to your congregation, I will appreciate it very much. I'm sending you a few good memories my wife and I had while ministering in Moscow.

When we knew I was being transferred to Moscow, Tencha (my wife), sent a letter to the Chamber of Commerce in Moscow. The Chairperson then was Anna Marie Webb (????). She answered my wife explaining that Moscow was a very small town with only three hundred people. No Chamber of Commerce! I drove to Moscow first and then went back for my family. The first thing I noticed when I entered Kansas was that most people driving in the highway waved at me, so I said, "This must be a very friendly country." Then I began to smell the thousands and thousands of cattle, which I didn't mind being a meat eater. As I arrived in town the first member of the church I met was Ashley Slemp. She was selling fireworks in a booth by the side of the highway. She asked me if I was the new pastor. I said yes. Then I met Nicole, Ashley's sister, walking in the middle of the street.

Some of the good memories that I have from this church (among many others) are the youth sitting in the first pews during the worship services, the children, the time we took the confirmation class to an Afro-American UMC in Wichita, the Christmas we went caroling singing "Feliz Navidad" (among others). I don't want to forget the meals and the home-made biscuits made by the "chefs" of the church and Avis Curtis' cinnamon rolls and the fellowship we had, the Ground Hog Days, and I haven't forgotten Mark Horyna when he made me cry (when I was by myself) in the last PPRC meeting when I announced that I was being transferred to the Rio Grande Conference. The District

Superintendent Dennis Couger (?) asked, "What can we do?" Mark responded, "Let's clone him." There I realized the mistake I have made by asking for a transfer.

Please let Carl Brollier know that I don't have a secretary...yet, but that I'm working on it.

Some regrets: Not being able to participate more in the sport youth games; not staying long enough. A Big thanks to all the people who loaded the truck when I moved.

May God bless you and keep you. If we don't see you again, make sure we'll meet again in heaven

Josué and Hortensia Mora.

"For by grace you have been saved through faith,
and that not of yourselves;
it is the gift of God, not of works, lest anyone should boast."
Ephesians 2:8-9

The season of Advent is probably the most anticipated holiday season for many Christians seconded only to the season of Lent with the celebration of our Lords resurrection on Easter Morning. But, it is the season of Advent that announces the birth of our Savior, Jesus Christ.

The season of Advent begins the four Sundays prior to Christmas and culminates on Christmas Eve. At this point, Christmastide begins and lasts until Epiphany, which is on January 6. Christmastide, you may know as "the twelve days of Christmas" because it lasts for twelve days beginning with the day after Christmas.

Advent is the time in which present day Christians wait for Christ's return.

"'And in the last days it shall be, God declares,
that I will pour out my Spirit on all flesh,
and your sons and your daughters shall prophesy, and your young men
shall see visions, and your old men shall dream dreams;"
Acts 2:17

Hallelujah!!!

These two rejoicing angels are currently spreading the news of Christ's birth in front of the United Methodist Church of Moscow. The 18 and a half foot-tall statues are the work of welder Dick Trahern of Turpin, Ok.

The concept of designing the angels came from church member Jan Rae Lewis who saw a similar pair of angels in front of a residence in Liberal. She talked to the lady of the home hoping to find out who made them but received no cooperation.

Undaunted, Jan Rae wrote authorities at the Rockefeller Center which has it's own angels of that type. The center sent her pictures and information about the construction. With this in hand Jan Rae con-tacted Wayne Comer who is in charge of the memorials at the church and asked him if he'd be interested in having two angels assembled. "He said he'd love to", she says.

Jan Rae called Dick, a former member of the Moscow community and he was enthusiastic about the project. He welded iron strips together into the design and they secured some brass horns for the final touch.

The twin trumpeters will be part of the Moscow Methodists' Christmas decorations in the future. If you hurry you can catch a glimpse of them before they take them down in January.

(Hugoton Hermes, 1992)

"The church is in a similar situation to Israel at the end of the Old Testament: in exile, waiting and hoping in prayerful expectation for the coming of the Messiah. Israel looked back to God's past gracious actions on their behalf in leading them out of Egypt in the Exodus, and on this basis they called for God once again to act for them. In the same way, the church, during Advent, looks back upon Christ's coming in celebration while at the same time looking forward in eager anticipation to the coming of Christ's kingdom when he returns for his people." (Holcomb, 2014)

Within this anticipation of our Saviors return, we anxiously await the angelic announcement. Moscow United Methodist Church demonstrates this with the eighteen and one half feet tall lit angels. In the image above you can see the interesting story of how these figures came to town through the efforts of Jan Rae Lewis, Wayne Comer, and former Moscowite: welder Dick Trahern from Turpin, Oklahoma.

(Hugoton Hermes, 1992)

So, since 1991 each year during Advent and Christmastide, the angels stand tall and proud in the front lawn of the church trumpeting for the faithful to O Come, O Come, Emanuel.

Wayne Comer

As with joy, sadness is with us and in 2008, Moscow lost one of its most endearing members. Wayne Comer or Mr. Comer as he was always called passed away in his home. He was very active in the church, playing the organ, chairing the Pastor Parish Committee, Administrative Council member, and teacher of the "Older Adult" Sunday school class. He played for many funerals and weddings and even made a CD, which the congregation has cherished since his death. While he never married or had a family of his own, according to Mr. Comer, it did not matter, because he always called the schoolchildren his kids. Mr. Comer was born July 12, 1927 and died May 28, 2008. He was loved and respected by so many that the school had to open the gymnasium for his funeral and it was packed.

Mr. Comer had many contributions to the town of Moscow, the church, and furthering his service to the Lord, including a song he wrote for the 75th anniversary of the church. It is titled HAPPY ANNIVERSARY.

This song was composed and written for Moscow United Methodist Church's 75th anniversary:

Opening: HAPPY ANNIVERSARY! You have reached your diamond year, that's the reason on this day we all are gathered here. To advance His Kingdom in our community – HAPPY, HAPPY ANNIVERSARY!

1. In the year of 1913 a faithful Christian band,
Built a little church for service on this prairie land.
A white frame church dedicated to God, and some are here today
Who served that church so faithfully in times long passed away.
Every Sunday morning, Ida Shriver as a rule;

5-30-08

Wayne Comer

MOSCOW – Wayne Comer, 80, died May 28, 2008. He was born July 12, 1927, in Fay, Okla., son of Alfred and Violet Gillespie Comer. He was a teacher for 42 and a half years.

He belonged to United Methodist Church, where he had been the organist and chancel choir director.

Survivors include: brother-in-law, Don Hill, Liberal; sister-in-law, Shirley Comer, Calumet, Okla.; and numerous nephews and nieces.

Funeral will be at 2 p.m. Monday in the Wayne Comer Gymnasium, Moscow. Friends may call from 2 to 8 p.m. Sunday at Paul's Funeral Home, Hugoton. Burial will be at 11 a.m. Tuesday in Mt. Hope Cemetery, Fay, Okla. Memorials to: United Methodist Church, Moscow, or Wayne Comer Scholarship Fund, both in care of the mortuary.

Rang the church bell early in announcing Sunday school.
Fourteen pastors served the church in many a by-gone day,
And therefore after 75 years, we gather here to say. (Chorus)

2. *By the year of 1928 the membership all knew.*
The little church must be replaced as the congregation grew.
And so the basement church was built and served so very well,
And on a tower behind this church was placed the cherished bell.
At last the church had classroom space and bathrooms new and clean
Best of all – its kitchen space; the likes had ne'er been seen.
Thus began the church Bazaars and Harvest dinners, too;
The work continues yet today and now we say to you. (Chorus)

3. *In the early 1950's it was evident to all.*
The church had grown in membership, again 'twas much too small.
The official board began to plan in sessions held with prayer.
As a result we're here today to show we truly care.
And as the church bell on this roof has served all churches three;
So many our lives ring out for Christ in service faithfully.
As we still take up the work from those who've gone before.
With humble hearts and joyful sound, the theme echoes once more.

Chorus: HAPPY ANNIVERSARY! We're proud of you today;
HAPPY ANNIVERSARY! We'll help in any way.
And with God's hand to guide us, in service we shall see
Advancement of His Kingdom here through many years to be

Final Cadenza: And so today we simply say:
HAPPY, HAPPY, HAPPY, ANNIVERSARY! TO OUR CHURCH!

Zo Ann Roland, Choir Accompanist and Church Pianist. Wayne Comer, Organist and Choir Director.

(Photograph taken from 75th Anniversary Directory)

They spoke and said to King Nebuchadnezzar, "O king, live forever! You, O king, have made a decree that everyone who hears the sound of the horn, flute, harp, lyre, and psaltery, in symphony with all kinds of music, shall fall down and worship the gold image; and whoever does not fall down and worship shall be cast into the midst of a burning fiery furnace. There are certain Jews whom you have set over the affairs of the province of Babylon: Shadrach, Meshach, and Abed-Nego; these men, O king, have not paid due regard to you. They do not serve your gods or worship the gold image which you have set up."

Then Nebuchadnezzar, in rage and fury, gave the command to bring Shadrach, Meshach, and Abed-Nego. So they brought these men before the king. Nebuchadnezzar spoke, saying to them, "Is it true, Shadrach, Meshach, and Abed-Nego, that you do not serve my gods or worship the gold image which I have set up? Now if you are ready at the time you hear the sound of the horn, flute, harp, lyre, and psaltery, in symphony with all kinds of music, and you fall down and worship the image which I have made, good! But if you do not worship, you shall be cast immediately into the midst of a burning fiery furnace. And who is the god who will deliver you from my hands?"

Daniel 3:9 – 15

There is a picture book written by Claire Huchet Bishop entitled *The Five Chinese Brothers.* It tells the story of five identical Chinese brothers. Each of the brothers has a unique gift that no one ever knew about, but their family. One could suck up the entire sea into his cheeks and hold it there for a while, another could stretch his legs to great lengths, one had a neck of steel, one could hold his breath forever and the last could not be burned.

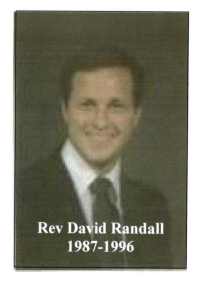
Rev David Randall
1987-1996

One day, a child who had watched one brother brings home many fish. He begged to go with him to learn his fishing secrets. Through no fault of the brothers the boy drowned because he refused to come to the shore when the brother could not hold the sea water any longer. Subsequently the brother was charged in the boy's death and was sentenced to death himself. One by one, each of the brothers secretively took the place of their brother and survived all attempts to kill him.

A cute story, yet not very believable. However, in the bible story of Shadrach, Meshach, and Abed-Nego, we hear a similar story.

"Shadrach, Meshach, and Abed-Nego answered and said to the king, "O Nebuchadnezzar, we have no need to answer you in this matter. If that is the case, our God whom we serve is able to deliver us from the burning fiery furnace, and He will deliver us from your hand, O king. But if not, let it be known to you, O king, that we do not serve your gods, nor will we worship the gold image which you have set up."
Daniel 3:16 – 18

Shadrach, Meshach, and Abed-Nego were servants of the Lord, not fictional other gods. They trusted in God to deliver them one way or the other. If they were not burned, they would be saved, if they were burned alive, their vindication came in Glory. They would be with God.

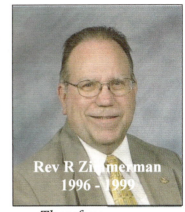

Rev R Zimmerman
1996 - 1999

Then Nebuchadnezzar was full of fury, and the expression on his face changed toward Shadrach, Meshach, and Abed-Nego. He spoke and commanded that they heat the furnace seven times more than it was usually heated. And he commanded certain mighty men of valor who were in his army to bind Shadrach, Meshach, and Abed-Nego, and cast them into the burning fiery furnace. Then these men were bound in their coats, their trousers, their turbans, and their other garments, and were cast into the midst of the burning fiery furnace. Therefore, because the king's command was urgent, and the furnace exceedingly hot, the flame of the fire killed those men who took up Shadrach, Meshach, and Abed-Nego. And these three men, Shadrach, Meshach, and Abed-Nego, fell down bound into the midst of the burning fiery furnace.

Then King Nebuchadnezzar was astonished; and he rose in haste and spoke, saying to his counselors, "Did we not cast three men bound into the midst of the fire?"

They answered and said to the king, "True, O king."

"Look!" he answered, "I see four men loose, walking in the midst of the fire; and they are not hurt, and the form of the fourth is like the Son of God."

Rev William Ripley
2001 - 2004

Then Nebuchadnezzar went near the mouth of the burning fiery furnace and spoke, saying, "Shadrach, Meshach, and Abed-Nego, servants of the Most High God, come out, and come here." Then Shadrach, Meshach, and Abed-Nego came from the midst of the fire, And the satraps, administrators, governors, and the king's counselors gathered together, and they saw these men on whose bodies the fire had no power; the hair of their head was not singed nor were their garments affected, and the smell of fire was not on them.

Nebuchadnezzar spoke, saying, "Blessed be the God of Shadrach, Meshach, and Abed-Nego, who sent His Angel and delivered His servants who trusted in Him, and they have frustrated the king's word, and yielded their bodies, that they should not serve nor worship any god except their own God!

Daniel 3:19-28

Nebuchadnezzar orders the three to be burned to death in a fire seven times the normal heat. However, when Shadrach, Meshach, and Abed-Nego were put into the fiery furnace, they were not consumed! Why? Because it was not in God's plan, God had something else in mind and it included the redemption of Nebuchadnezzar soul.

These types of miracles are a little harder to recognize today. They seem to be a little more subtle, or many even call these subtle miracles…a coincidence, but, are they?

On a Sunday morning in the winter of 2011, the congregation noticed that it was a little bit cooler than normal in the sanctuary, however, it was an extremely cold morning and 'after all, we do have high ceilings and heat does rise." The thermostat was turned up and the worship service continued.

By Wednesday it was still cooler than it should have been, almost cold, especially in the fellowship hall where Kids Club was going on. The forty plus grade school kids did not seem to notice, but Pastor Tim felt he should check out why the sudden lack of heat. After checking the vents, it appeared that the problem was with the blowers and a repairman needed to be called. "The repairman is out of town until Monday" the Pastor reported, "I'll call again the first of the week."

Four days later on Sunday morning the faint smell of smoke could be detected. Not many seemed to notice, so, "It's probably nothing." Still, the heat was not working and the congregation began talking about where they could hold services next week if it could not be repaired.

The next day when the repairman was called again, he said he was not available until later in the week. "It seems everyone's heater went on the fritz while I was on vacation" he said.

Tuesday morning the sanctuary was full of smoke! Looking around, Pastor Tim could not find the source so decided to take a look at the furnace. What he saw made his heart jump into his throat. The furnace had apparently been on fire for some time! Even though the fellowship hall was still full of smoke, the fire was out and the interior of the furnace was cold.

The gas stoves in the kitchen are old and the pilot lights were always lit. The fire could have created an explosion and people could have been hurt or even killed. The beautiful church with that old bell could have been reduced to rubble if it was not for the hand of God. Especially frightening was the very real concern for the children because Kids Club was held in the fellowship hall…right next to the kitchen.

More than likely the fire had been burning during the worship service. Praise God, for His miracles and praise Him again for sparing the church members and especially the children whose faith grew a little more that year.

A Few Words from Rev. Roy Nelson (2004-2006)

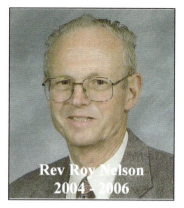

A good many years ago some advertisements caught my attention in a special way. Basic to any advertising campaign is the need to first gain the attention of the public and then to lead us to act. When companies are willing to spend tens of millions and more in advertising, it is certain they have looked deep into which might compel a buyer to notice and then act. Certain ads have led me to think they are trying to answer some need, some hunger much deeper than the product might logically meet.

The first one I noticed (and you can tell this was years ago) was a car that was, "Something to believe in." Buicks may be a very nice car, but was General Motors trying to sell a car, based on a deep feeling in the nation which sensed a loss of some of our "roots." Was there a loss of the things we once believed in? That ad is in the distant past in ad history. A current example is a car that is made with "love." I do not know which parts are made with love; however I can identify where steel, plastics, rubber, copper, glass and other ingredients may be found. Is there a feeling of loneliness, isolation and lovelessness, in a nation where cars can be sold because they are made with love? In addition, the existence of all the dating sites being advertised, seem to be asking the same question.

I have been wondering as I have watched many different kinds of television programs, if advertising is going to be taken over by attorneys offering to sue for any number of things. To be certain, part of the appeal in their message is the money, often quoting enormous amounts. There also seems to be another message as well, "Who is responsible for what has happened to me," "How can they be punished?"

I offer two more examples; you may have others in mind. The first example made me think of many of the westerns I have watched. There was often a scene where one of the characters pours his needed courage out of a bottle. Recently one of the largest soft drink companies has been suggesting if you are a student called to make a presentation, best man at a wedding about to offer remarks, a teacher facing a class room or even a famous performer about to go onstage, courage and ability to meet those challenges comes from their soft drink. One last example, there is a punch line from an old ad which keeps reappearing in different ways. "Where's the beef," seems to be asking about real substance in a society that is so often superficial. All these examples leads me to suggest, you look for windows into the human soul, often found in ads for some of the deeper hungers, they are artificially trying to fill.

Last and most important, let me suggest the bell of the Moscow congregation has rung in answer to the deepest of human hungers and needs. It has lifted hope; it has offered the ultimate one to believe in. It has called people to a community where the love and acceptance of others is found, AND the assurance of the unending love of our creator is assured. It has offered some answers to the haunting questions of why some things happen in life and the strength to continue when there seem to be no answers. The bell has called people to, and remains a symbol of, what is most important in life so no one needs to look back on their life and ask about their days, "Where's the beef?"

Strange isn't it, a hundred years plus of doing these things on just a street corner, in a small community, in a corner of a state often looked down on by the élite, knows more about some of the answers of life's deepest needs.   (Nelson)

Halloween is not always a favorite holiday among Christians. The idea of children dressing up as ghosts and goblins has an evil ring to it and something many would rather not participate.

Halloween, in of its self, is a tradition that has been around since "its origins in the ancient Celtic festival known as Samhain (pronounced "sah-win")" (History of Halloween, 2014) It is a pagan holiday for sure, but what does the bible say about it?

The bible condemns actions having to do with witchcraft or the occult. Deuteronomy tells us:

> *"There shall not be found among you anyone who makes his son or his*
> *daughter pass through the fire,*
> *or one who practices witchcraft, or a soothsayer,*
> *or one who interprets omens, or a sorcerer,*
> *or one who conjures spells, or a medium, or a spiritist,*
> *or one who calls up the dead.*
> *For all who do these things are an abomination to the L*ORD*,*
> *and because of these abominations*
> *the L*ORD *your God drives them out from before you."*
> Deuteronomy 18:10-12

As for participating in the gala activities of Halloween, it does not include practicing witchcraft, sacrificing sons and daughters or interpreting omens. Halloween in our traditions today that includes dressing up in costumes, going door to door calling out "Trick or Treat", collecting enough candy to choke a horse, and getting sick enough on that candy to stay home from school the next day.

Some sources say that the Pagans believed that the door to allow evil in to roam the earth looking for people to hurt was on Halloween, October 31st of each year. In order to not be the target of one of these evil ones, it was believed that you were to wear a  costume that would fool those that were intent on harm they would leave you alone. It was also believed that if you left some sort of gift in the form of cake or other goodies outside your front door, those evil doers would take the confectioners and leave you alone.

In response to this tradition, the church began to observe November 1st as "All Saints Day", beginning at midnight. It is said that at midnight each Halloween, all the saints in Heaven come to earth and banish all the evil back to hell.

The holiday is a favorite among some and a burden among others. You can find gaiety at parties with dunking for apples, smoking punch, and candied popcorn balls or you can find stick pins in candy bars intent to harm.

In the late 1960's, needle's were reportedly found in apples from one residence sparking parents concern and disgust everywhere. Parents began checking their children's cache throwing any treat found unwrapped, homemade, or with suspicious  pin holes. From the beginning, Halloween has and still continues to be fraught with trouble. Still children want to go out, and parents want to allow them to go. Today, more and more parents go out with their children, for safety and the security that their children will not go anywhere that might hurt them. They continue to check their kids' candy for suspicious pieces and homemade treats from houses they do not know.

In 2006 Moscow United Methodist adopted a program that would not only make the night of Halloween safer for the kids, but would also bring more glory to the Father. The program was "Trunk or Treat". This program was not for Methodist's only, but for the entire community of Moscow. Those who wished to participate would bring their vehicle to the church. They would decorate their trunk and the children would come and parade up and down the line of trunks trick or treating. Parents were assured their children were safe and the treats were equally safe.

"Bear one another's burdens, and so fulfill the law of Christ."
Galatians 6:2

MOSCOW METHODIST CHURCH
Bervie A. Scott, Pastor.

Next Sunday:
Church school meets at 10 a.m.
Mrs. J. M. Shriver, Supt.
Morning worship begins at 11:00 a. m. Sermon theme: "The Value of Christianity."
Methodist Men's Hour on KSCB at 2:00 p. m.
Church covered dish supper beginning at 6:30 p. m. The program will include Inauguration pictures, song service, special talent, and worship service. Plan now to attend and bring your friends.
Friday, February 20:
The W.S.C.S. will observe "The World Day of Prayer" with a covered dish dinner being served at noon and the program following. Everyone is invited.

Rev. Scott and family ate supper with the Carl Brollier family last Sunday evening.
Rev and Mrs. Scott attended the sub-district ministers' monthly luncheon and business meeting at the Johnson Methodist Church last Monday.
Mrs. B. A. Scott was hostess to W S.C.S. circle I Thursday afternoon Feb 12.

In this Hugoton Hermes article dated February 19, 1953 (page 3) Pastor Scott announces church school, morning worship, as well as other church activities including the celebration of World Day of Prayer and that the Women of W.S.C.S. planned to observe with a 'covered dish dinner' and a program.

UPDATE: Moscow, KS Residents Allowed To Return Home

Thursday, May 30, 2013

Residents of the small southwest Kansas town of Moscow have been allowed to return home, after being evacuated overnight.

A fire has been burning since early Wednesday, and winds shifted overnight, leading to the precautionary evacuation. At about 3:30 a.m., A temporary

shelter was set up at Hugoton High School, where Red Cross set up cots for people to sleep.

People were allowed to return home around 9 a.m.

Wednesday, May 29, 2013

A large fire continues to burn in southwest Kansas, and investigators believe the blaze was intentionally set.

According KSCB Radio, it began around midnight as a grass fire in Stevens County near the co-op in Moscow. The fire has since spread and now involves 50,000 corn stalk bales.

Moscow Mayor Billy Bell told KAKE News that firefighters have it contained, and

that local farms have their irrigation wells on standby to assist if needed. No evacuations have been issued, but the mayor said residents have been told to prepare just in case the wind changes.

The bales on fire are stored north of town at a facility owned by Agengno Bioenergy and were to be used for ethanol production. The fire is large in area, but the mayor said no structures are currently in danger.

Investigators believe arson is to blame. No injuries have been reported, but the fire could burn as long as two to three weeks.

http://www.kake.com/home/headlines/Large-Fire-Continues-To-Burn-In-SW-Kansas-209344921.html

(Kake.com, 2014)

"The Lord also will be a refuge for the oppressed,
A refuge in times of trouble."
Psalm 9:9

It was approximately 11:00 pm on May 28, 2013 when the smell of smoke, once more, filled the air. This time the smoke came from outside. As people ventured outside to see what was going on, the sounds of fire engines could be heard in the distance. Police officers were going from door to door, telling everyone they could find, "There is a fire on the west side of the tracks, it is blowing this way, you may want to see if you can go stay somewhere else."

Many Moscowites left fearing for their safety. Some stayed behind including Pastor Tim McCrary and the Reverend Larry Bradford from the Baptist church. Pastor Tim decided to open the Methodist Church and to also help the police alert the town to the fire. The next day, May 29th, it was reported by KSN TV that 60,000 bales of hay (approximately 1,000 lbs each) was burning and the fire was not letting up. In fact, in the early morning hours of the third day, May 30th, the police were once again going door to door telling those they could raise, there had been a shift in the wind and it was extremely advised to evacuate the town. Again, many left, yet some stayed.

The Moscow United Methodist church was opened up for anyone working on the fire or those willing to lend a hand in feeding, housing, and even charging cell phones, if that was what they needed. The Hugoton High School opened up a temporary shelter for those who had nowhere to go and the Moscow high school opened so any of the emergency personnel could shower since they were on 24 hour duty. Members of the church along with other volunteers took meals, drinks, and snacks to the command center for those who could not take timeout to come to the church for rest and food. Pastor Larry from the Baptist Church joined Pastor Tim tirelessly aiding and serving the many workers trying to save the little town. Once again the two Moscow churches joined forces in a time of need.

There were so many who felt God's nudge and asked; "how can I help?" People from as far away as Dodge City were showing up to serve, some did not even know anyone who lived in Moscow yet felt the call. People and businesses, near and far, brought pop, fruit, and Gatorade, whatever they could bring, was brought. Restaurants were sending complete meals to serve the firefighters and helpers. The Red Cross showed up with cot's blankets and small bags with toiletries to be passed out. Even FEMA stepped in to see if they were needed and all stayed until they were either totally exhausted or were no longer needed.

Firefighters worked day and night to put out the fire, unfortunately each time they would soak an area and go on to the next, a plume of fire would spark back up. The fire took weeks to totally burn out and the hay was a total loss. It had been determined that the only thing that could be done was to control the fire and let it burn itself out.
The little town of Moscow had seen more neighborly love, than some larger cities would ever see.

One of the parishioners wrote a letter to her cousin talking about the blessings from God the church had received in order to care for the many in need;

> "...I was at the church yesterday receiving food. Two Baptist sisters were with me. Our preacher went home to bed.....he's been up the last 2 nights keeping the church open for the 24 hour crew who would come in for a break thru out the night. The people of Hugoton have been flooding their little "sister city" with food and drinks. One company brought 25 cases of Gatorade and 25 cases of water....... Last

Do you smell smoke?

night, the Chamber of Commerce feed our little town with brisket. Tonight, we will have a huge dinner (400 expected) to share our stories and encourage one another. Early the first full day of this event, I was driving to town to help at church. It was daybreak. The town lights were still on (low on the horizon) and there was a thick cloud of smoke hovering over Moscow. Then, all of a sudden, I saw a light shining in the dark smoke. It was up high and shining thru the cloud of smoke. It was quite a site. I praised God for this beautiful view of His Sovereignty.....in the midst of the storm, our Lord and our God is there, like a light shining in the darkness. This light was the elevator light, but you won't convince me other than it being a beautiful promise from God that He is with us at all times." (Lahey, 2013)

> *"Jesus said to him, 'you shall love the LORD your God with all your heart, with all your soul, and with all your mind. This is the first and great commandment. And the second is like it: 'You shall love your neighbor as yourself. On these two commandments hang all the Law and the Prophets."*
> Matthew 22:37-41

Those who came because of the call included: Stevens County, Morton County, Haskell County, Grant County, Kearney County, Finney County, Seward County, Texas County, Beaver County, Ford County, Meade County, Gray County, Stanton County, City of Garden City, City of Liberal, City of Hugoton, City of Moscow, Red Cross, FEMA, Homeland

Security, Emergency management, The Store, Moscow Schools, SW Region Incident, Management Team, Antlers Restaurant, Black Hills Energy, Moscow Fire Station, XI ETA ALPHA Sorority, Hugoton Chamber of Commerce, Fiss Architecture Design, Hugoton Dollar Store, Whites Foods, 1st National Bank, Citizens State Bank, Hugoton Fire Station, Abengoa, B&B Harper Farms, Hugoton Hermes Newspaper, Ramsey Insurance, Hugoton Rotary, Wolters Construction, Rome Farms, Young Trucking, American Implement, Flamingo Motel, Hancock Electric, and those who did not leave their name.

13 counties, 4 cities, and 30 businesses and emergency aid organizations, in all.

Some words from Pastor Tim McCrary:

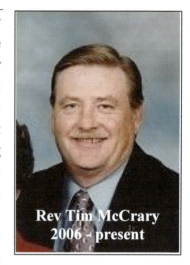

Rev Tim McCrary
2006 - present

"Greetings in Christ's Name. Well, our community has once more suffered an ordeal that could have turned tragic at the "whim of the wind", yet through our faith in God and love of neighbor we are getting through it with flying colors (and some ash). Isn't rural life great! Especially if we are surrounded by such great neighbors. How many times did I hear from those living out of town, "If the town is evacuated and anyone asks where to go, send them out to me." Or, "Pastor, what do you need; how can I help?"

You see, since most of us do not have the expertise, the resources, or even the physical ability to do what the firefighters and command personnel do, we cannot do their job. But we can do our job, the job of being disciples of a Savior who calls us to serve all. To do this job (or should I say to do this way of life) we use what God gives us, whether it be monetary gifts or servant gifts (like gifts of the Holy Spirit). We who were there saw this type of thing happening over and over again.

Gifts poured in from all over, people from surrounding towns coming in with grocery sacks full, vehicles pilled with needed items such as drinks and food. Phone calls were plentiful with offers of help. Soon after a need was posted on Facebook it arrived. As I write this, I am sitting at the church waiting on another shift of firefighters to come in to eat. Where I sit I can see four coolers full of pop and water, two tables and two counters completely full of food and snacks including six cakes, tons of cookies, and 39 cases of different kinds of soda. All these items were brought by caring 'neighbors'. Also with me are about eight people waiting to help, some of them not even a part of our church, although a part of the Church Universal. Pastor and Toni Bradford from the Baptist Church were constantly here also serving and being good Christian examples for us all. That, my friends, is the way it is supposed to be. Jesus called what we are doing love of neighbor, meaning that in times of trouble, family/community comes together to help each other."

"Then the King will say to those on His right hand, 'Come, you blessed of My Father, inherit the kingdom prepared for you from the foundation of the world: for I was hungry and you gave Me food; I was thirsty and you gave Me drink; I was a stranger and you took Me in; I was naked and you clothed Me; I was sick and you visited Me; I was in prison and you came to Me."
Matthew 25:34-36

The Moscow United Methodist Church has seen many changes, some good, and some bad. They have gone through fire, crime, dirt storms, war, poverty, and prosperity. But the one thing that never changed and was a constant presence in all things, was God. Life changes, styles change, people, and relationships change, but God and his love for all remains the same.

Part V

LORD OF THE DANCE

I danced in the morning when the world was begun,
And I danced in the moon and the stars and the sun,
And I came down from heaven and I danced on the earth,
   At Bethlehem I had my birth.

   Dance, then, wherever you may be;
   I am the Lord of the Dance, said he.
  And I'll lead you all wherever you may be,
  And I'll lead you all in the dance, said he.

   I danced for the scribe and the Pharisee,
But they would not dance and they would not follow me;
 I danced for the fishermen, for James and John;
   They came to me and the dance went on.

   Dance, then, wherever you may be;
   I am the Lord of the Dance, said he.
  And I'll lead you all wherever you may be,
  And I'll lead you all in the dance, said he.

I danced on a Friday and the sky turned black;
It's hard to dance with the devil on your back;
They buried my body and they thought I'd gone,
   But I am the dance and I still go on.

   They cut me down and I leapt up high,
   I am the life that'll never, never die;
   I'll live in you if you'll live in me;
   I am the Lord of the Dance, said he.

   Dance, then, wherever you may be;
   I am the Lord of the Dance, said he.
  And I'll lead you all wherever you may be,
  And I'll lead you all in the dance, said he.

   words by Sydney Carter 1963
      music is from: "Simple Gifts" by Elder Joseph Brackett, 1848

And so God blessed, that old bell
and all those that answered its call
He bless the members of that little frame church for the service
they gave to others
He blessed those in the basement church for the love they freely gave
And He blessed all those members of the new brick church whose faith
and love in that Risen Savior and the Father has grown with each day.
God has blessed the community of Moscow and because
of His Call and the Answer to
Servant Hood
Love of Neighbor
and Faith in His Saving Grace

And That Old Bell rings on ...

Bulletin for the 100th year celebration Sunday

Moscow United Methodist Church
100 Year Celebration
November 3, 2013
Order of Service

Call to Worship
"Sing Hallelujah"
The Bell quartet - The Junior Choir -
The Moscow Chancel Choir - The Congregation
Sing Hallelujah to the King
Sing Hallelujah, let it ring.
Sing Hallelujah, don't be late,
Today is the Day we celebrate.

Announcements and Birthdays

Celebration In Music
Jacob Bell
"Surely the Presence of the Lord Is In This Place"   328
Choir - "Happy Anniversary"

Lifting Up Our Prayers For the Next 100 Years
Celebrating With the Children

Scripture and Meditation

Sharing Our Tithes and Gifts

The Re-consecration of the Moscow United Methodist Church
Holy Communion

"We Are the Church"   558

Benediction

After we eat we will all come back to the Sanctuary for more celebration - With
messages from former pastors, music by Jan Reece and the Moscow Baptist Hillbilly
Band - as well as Rhea Horyna, who will play some of her songs for us. Hope you can
stay.
A Service for the Re -consecration of our Church

Brothers and sisters in Christ, this is a day of rejoicing. We are here today to celebrate 110 years of ministry and to re-consecrate this building of the Moscow United Methodist Church. Let us open our hearts and minds to receive God's Word with faith. May our blessed communion, born of one baptism and nurtured at one table of the Lord, become one temple of the Holy Spirit as we gather in love.

By what name shall this house be known

It shall be called the Moscow United Methodist Church.

Dear friends, rejoice that God so moved the hearts of people that this house has been built for praise and prayer. Let us now re-consecrate it for service and celebrate its holy use.

O eternal God, mighty in power and of incomprehensible majesty, whom the heavens cannot contain, much less the walls of temples made with hands, you have promised your special presence whenever two or three are assembled in your name to offer praise and prayer.

By the power of your Holy Spirit re-consecrate this house of your worship. Bless us and sanctify what we do here, that this place may be holy for us and a house of prayer for all people.

Guide and empower in this place by the same Spirit the proclamation of your word and the celebration of your Sacraments, the pouring out of prayer and the singing of your praise, professions of faith and testimonies to your grace, the joining of men and women in marriage and the celebration of death and resurrection.

Save us from that failure of vision which would confine out worship within these walls, but send us out from here to be your servants in the world, sharing the blessings of Christ with the world he came to redeem.

O God, sanctify this place for everything in and on earth is yours. Yours, Lord, is the dominion, and you are exalted as head above all.

Lord, your Word is a lantern to our feet and a light upon our path. We re-consecrate this pulpit in the name of the Father and of the Son and of the Holy Spirit. Amen.

Lord, there is one faith, one baptism, one God and Father of us all. We re-consecrate this baptismal font in the name of the Father, and of the Son, and of the Holy Spirit. Amen.

Lord God, we thank you that when we gather at the Lord's table the living Christ is known to us in the breaking of the bread and the sharing of the cup; and we are renewed as His body, whose life is in His blood. We re-consecrate this table in the name of the Father, and of the Son, and of the Holy Spirit. Amen.

I SERVE A RISEN SAVIOR

I serve a risen Savior
He's in the world today.
I know that He is living,
Whatever men may say.
I see His hand of mercy;
I hear His voice of cheer;
And just the time I need Him
He's always near.
He lives, He lives, Christ Jesus lives today!
He walks with me and talks with me along life's narrow way.
He lives, He lives, salvation to impart!
You ask me how I know He lives?
He lives within my heart.
In all the world around me
I see His loving care,
And though my heart grows weary,
I never will despair;
I know that He is leading,
Through all the stormy blast;
The day of His appearing
Will come at last.
Rejoice, rejoice, O Christian,
Lift up your voice and sing
Eternal hallelujahs
To Jesus Christ the King!
The Hope of all who seek Him,
The Help of all who find,
None other is so loving,
So good and kind.

Words by Alfred Henry Ackley (1887-1960) Music by Alfred Henry Ackley (1887-1960)

Source: http://www.hymnal.net/en/hymn/h/503#ixzz32aw7Nd2H

I AM THE CHURCH! YOU ARE THE CHURCH!

I am the church! You are the church!
We are the church together!
All who follow Jesus,
all around the world!
Yes, we're the church together!

The church is not a building;
the church is not a steeple;
the church is not a resting place;
the church is a people.

I am the church! You are the church!
We are the church together!
All who follow Jesus,
all around the world!
Yes, we're the church together!

We're many kinds of people,
with many kinds of faces,
all colours and all ages, too
from all times and places.

I am the church! You are the church!
We are the church together!
All who follow Jesus,
all around the world!
Yes, we're the church together!

And when the people gather,
there's singing and there's praying;
there's laughing and there's crying
sometimes,
all of it saying:

I am the church! You are the church!
We are the church together!
All who follow Jesus,
all around the world!
Yes, we're the church together!

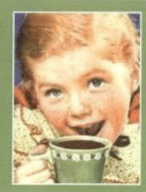

Fun sign in the kitchen for a while 2013

Easter egg hunt 2013

Holly Smith   2013

Vacation Bible

School Marshmallow fun 2013

Kids Club Graduates 2013

KIDS WILL BE KIDS, all of them…

When the children would come up to the front of the church for Young Disciples Time the Pastor thought it might be fun if he was to challenge the children to fill a bucket with coins. The coins would go to feed the children. The money collected would go to three different funds that dealt with feeding children.

Pastor Tim challenged the children to fill the bucket by the end of Lent and if they could, he would let them cut his hair. It was a large bucket, about four or five gallons and he really did not think the children could fill it. But, just in case, he thought he better grow his hair out.

Pastor did not anticipate the enthusiasm the congregation would have, nor did he anticipate to what great lengths the members would go to ensure his hair would get cut!

Well by the last Sunday in Lent, the bucket was full. The amount that went to the charity was well over $500.00 and Pastor Tim got "his ears lowered".

Pastor's a little worried, the kids won the challenge to cut his hair.

Praise God from whom all Blessing flow-

Jace Dale taking a picture with his phone.

Holly Smith on Ash Wednesday

The Baptist Hillbilly Band

Methodist Church Bazaar   Hugoton Hermes February 7, 2013

Memories, memories, and more precious memories.

Vacation Bible School

Party, party, party

Children's Choir

Confirmation Class graduates

Vacation Bible School

Choir singing the Cantata

(Hugoton Hermes, 1994)

"See you at the Pole"

"Then one of the scribes came, and having heard them reasoning together, perceiving[a] that He had answered them well, asked Him, "Which is the first commandment of all?"
Jesus answered him, "The first of all the commandments is: 'Hear, O Israel, the LORD our God, the LORD is one. And you shall love the LORD your God with all your heart, with all your soul, with all your mind, and with all your strength. This is the first commandment And the second, like it, is this: 'You shall love your neighbor as yourself. 'There is no other commandment greater than these." So the scribe said to Him, "Well said, Teacher. You have spoken the truth, for there is one God, and there is no other but He." Mark 12:28-32

Did you forget when school gets out again?

Kids Club

"When I was young, I asked the Lord 'why are we here'

and He told me "To love your neighbor"

So, That Old Bell continues to ring…

"Come to Me, all you who labor and are heavy laden, and I will give you rest."
                                            Matthew 11:28

Scripture

Deuteronomy 18:10-12

Psalm 61:1-4

Psalm 78:5-7

Ecclesiastes 2:24

Isaiah 40:28

Isaiah 41:10

Matthew 6:26

Matthew 11:28

Matthew 18:20

Matthew 19:14

Matthew 22:37-41

Matthew 25:35

Matthew 25:34-36

Mark 12:28-32

Luke 6:48

Luke 9:57

Luke 10:38-42

Luke 12:22-24

John 1:38-39

John 13:34-35

John 14.1

Acts 2:17

1 Chronicles 4:10

Galatians 6:2

Ephesians 2:8-9

Daniel 3:9 – 15

Daniel 3:16 – 18

Daniel 3:19-28

With special appearances by
<u>Micah and Malachi the church mice…</u>

All Bible verses taken from the NKJV translation

Bibliography

(n.d.).

(1913, March 7). *Hugoton Hermes*, p. 5.

1920, U. A. *Moscow Township, KS 1920.* Moscow.

(1921, April 20). *The Hugoton Hermes*, p. 7.

(1921, March 28). *Hugoton Hermes*, p. 7.

(1930, May 2). *The Hugoton Hermes*, p. 7.

Bigelow, W. (2014, 06 11). *The Failed U.S. Boycott of the 1980 Moscow Summer Olympics.* Retrieved from Global Research: http://www.globalresearch.ca/the-failed-u-s-boycott-of-the-1980-moscow-summer-olympics/5369121

Consultancy, W. C. (n.d.). *U.S. Population from 1900.* Retrieved from Demogrphia: http://www.census.gov/popclock/

History of Halloween. (2014, May 17). Retrieved from Safe Site Central, Inc.: HalloweenHistory.org

Holcomb, J. (2014, June 18). *What is Advent.* Retrieved from Christianity.com: http://www.christianity.com/christian-life/christmas/what-is-advent.html

Hugoton Hermes. (1931, 3 11).

Hugoton Hermes. (1931, October 30).

Hugoton Hermes. (1953, May 21). p. 1.

Hugoton Hermes. (1992, January 2). *Hallelujah!!*

Hugoton Hermes. (1994, September 29). p. 7.

I Serve a Risen Savior. (2014, May 23). Retrieved from Hymnal.net: http://www.hymnal.net/en/hymn/h/503

Jeremiah, D. (2014, March). High-definition Christian living. *Southwest Kansas Faith and Family*, pp. 34, 47.

Kake.com. (2014, 10 24). Retrieved from Kake.com: http://www.kake.com/home/headlines/Large-Fire-Continues-To-Burn-In-SW-Kansas-209344921.html

Kansas Historical Society. (2014). Retrieved from Kansas memory: http://www.kansasmemory.org/item/209526

Ken Curtis, P. (2014, May 25). *Christianity.com*. Retrieved from Whatever Happened to the Twelve Apostles?: http://www.christianity.com/church/church-history/timeline/1-300/whatever-happened-to-the-twelve-apostles-11629558.html

Lahey, P. (2013, May). e-mail letter to cousin. Moscow, KS.

LJM. *Micah and Malachi The Church Mice.*

McGill, S. (2014, May 21). (L. McCrary, Interviewer)

Miller, H. (2013). (P. a. McCrary, Interviewer) Moscow, KS: Documents and interviews.

MUMC. (1973). *United Methodist Church Moscow Kansas 1913 to 1973.* Wichita: Jeffrey's of Kansas.

Nelson, R. R. (n.d.).

Noob, S. (2014, May 17). *One in a million*. Retrieved from Ifish.net: http://www.ifish.net/board/showthread.php?t=217303

Patton, C. M. (2014, May 25). *Parchment and Pen*. Retrieved from What Happened to the Twelve Apostles? How Their Deaths Evidence Easter: http://www.reclaimingthemind.org/blog/2009/04/what-happened-to-the-twelve-apostles-how-their-deaths-evidence-easter/

ppt4web. (2014, April 5). Retrieved from Презентация на тему: Moscow in America: http://ppt4web.ru/anglijjskijj-jazyk/mosco-in-america.html

RexM, e. C. (2014). *eHow*. Retrieved March 28, 2014, from http://www.ehow.com/facts_6854087_difference-between-kerosene-coal-oil_.html

RexM, e. C. (n.d.). *eHow*.

Silver Beaver Award. (2014, June 3). Retrieved from Boy Scouts of America: http://www.scouting.org/scoutsource/awards_central/silverbeaver.aspx

SoftSchools.com. (n.d.). *1930's timeline*. Retrieved March 28, 2014, from http://www.softschools.com/terms_conditions.jsp

staff. (2014, 06 11). Moscow, Kansas offers. *Lawrence Journal-World*, p. 14.

Stevens County History Association. (1979). *The History of Stevens County & Its People.* The Lowell Press, Inc.

The Methodist Book Concern. (1916 - 1917, Jan - Nov). BARTEAU'S Sunday-School Record.

Unknown. (1974). *Scouting In Moscow.* Santa Fe Trail Echo.

Unknown. (n.d.). Dedication of Stained Glass Windows. Moscow, Kansas: hand typed.

Unknown, P. *Moscow Township 1920.* Moscow.

Venturio Media, LLP. (2012, October 28). *Dust Bowl Facts.* Retrieved from Great Depression
Facts: http://great-depression-facts.com/dust-bowl-facts/104/#sthash.eQD89iTt.dpuf,

Contributors to the publication of

That Old Bell

Lonnie & Ann Hess

Edria McCrary

June Lahey

United Methodist Women

City of Moscow

Stevens County Gas & Historical Museum

Elsie White

Garry & Zo Roland

Bill & Linda Harvey

Earl & Lonna Teeter

Sevalan Brollier

Shirley Mothes

Hazel Miller

Henry & Judy Cantrell

Nolan Megenity

And all God's children said...

"AMEN"